The Annotated Guide to Robert E. Howard's Weird Fantasy

Fred Blosser

Pulp Hero Press
The Most Dangerous Books on Earth
www.PulpHeroPress.com

Pulp Hero Press publishes its books in a variety of print and electronic formats. Some content that appears in one format may not appear in another.

Editor: Bob McLain
Layout: Artisanal Text
ISBN 978-1-68390-251-5
Printed in the United States of America
Pulp Hero Press | www.PulpHeroPress.com
Address queries to bob@pulpheropress.com

This book is dedicated In Memoriam to Thaddeus M. Dikty, Donald M. Grant, Glenn Lord, Jim Neal, and Robert E. Weinberg

Contents

Introduction:
Out of the Shadows

Once long ago, in a place far away...well, it seems long ago and far away now. In October 1976, I was contacted by Thaddeus M. (Ted) Dikty, a veteran science-fiction editor and publisher. Ted was in the midst of an ambitious publication program, initially through FAX Collector's Editions in partnership with Darrell C. Richardson and then through his own imprint, Starmont House, to publish the fiction of Robert E. Howard.

New readers were coming to Howard in great numbers through the Marvel comic magazines scripted by Roy Thomas, through paperback editions from Zebra Books with elegant Jeff Jones cover paintings, lavish hardcover collector's editions from FAX and Donald M. Grant, and small-circulation journals like Dennis McHaney's *The Howard Reader* and George T. Hamilton's *Cross Plains*. The late Glenn Lord was the indispensable figure who enabled this rising tide, as the pioneering Howard scholar and the tireless representative for the Howard literary properties. With this degree of audience enthusiasm, Ted saw a market not only *for* the stories of Conan, King Kull, Solomon Kane, and the rest, but also one for studies *about* this wonderful universe of swords, sorcery, and imagination.

Ted had just published one such work, *The Annotated Guide to Robert E. Howard's Sword & Sorcery* by Robert E. Weinberg, a well-known collector and expert. Ted was eager to publish a series of companion volumes, but Bob

was immersed in other projects, including the prepara-
tion of an authoritative history of *Weird Tales* magazine.
Meanwhile, I had established a sort of niche as a Howard
aficionado through articles in *The Howard Collector*, *Savage
Sword of Conan*, and other publications.

Ted asked if I'd like to prepare a volume in the same
format as Bob's *Annotated Guide*, covering Howard's work
in a different genre. If so, would I like to write about
Howard's weird fantasy work, or would I prefer to write
about his non-fantastic adventure stories?

I chose the weird fantasy theme, deciding that those
tales were the ones most likely to appeal to fans whose
taste for Howard's work had been whetted by Conan and
Kull. Ted agreed, adding an open invitation to proceed to
a further volume about REH's adventure heroes once I'd
wrapped up the project at hand. Over the next four months,
working around my day job and sending the manuscript
to Ted section by section to speed production, I wrote *The
Annotated Guide to Robert E. Howard's Weird Fantasy*.

Fate and Fortune

Ted listed the book as "forthcoming" in his 1977 catalogue
and then again in 1978. He even commissioned wonderful
cover art by Alex Nino, and set one section in type for
proofreading. But the Howard boom receded, Ted turned
to other endeavors, and *The Annotated Guide to Robert E.
Howard's Weird Fantasy* slipped into the limbo of unreal-
ized, specialty press projects—until now, thanks to the
opportunity offered by Bob McLain and Pulp Hero Press.

As new readers learn about Robert E. Howard, there
continues to be a use for reference works that explore the
worlds of Conan, Kull, Skull-Face, and the Black Stone.
The present book is intended to inform new fans who
continue to arrive at Howard's doorstep as we enter the
next decade of the twenty-first century, but I hope it will
also be of interest to veteran readers.

I've retained the format of Bob Weinberg's *The Annotated Guide to Robert E. Howard's Sword & Sorcery*, but refined and updated my original manuscript to take into account stories that have appeared since 1977, and to better reflect the body of scholarship and analytical criticism around Howard's fiction that began to accrue in earnest in the 1980s. I've assigned Howard's weird fantasies into categories that appear to be the most appropriate for grouping tales with common characters or themes:

- Cthulhu Mythos
- The Little People
- Gaelic Fear
- Ghosts
- Science Fiction
- Texas Terrors
- Swampland Shadows
- Skull-Face
- De Montour
- Jungle Horror
- Faring Town
- Psychic Investigators
- Shudder Stories

Cthulhu or Not?

Some of the weird fantasies overlap from one category into another, for Howard was rarely content to employ a theme without exploring all of its implications and associations. This can raise complications in assigning a given story to one category or another. For example, is "The Children of the Night" more properly included under "Cthulhu Mythos" or under "The Little People"?

In such cases, I have assigned the given story to the classification to which it I feel most strongly pertains, while noting its relevance to other segments of Howard's fiction on which it touches. Under this logic, I've placed "The Children of the Night" under the "Little People" heading while noting its relevance to the Cthulhu Mythos. In each section, the stories surveyed are listed in order of publication.

Howard's lasting reputation rests on his secure recognition as a pioneering master of sword-and-sorcery. However, he had a keen appreciation for weird fantasy and horror, and his first stories were published in *Weird Tales* magazine, among whose readers he remained a steady favorite even beyond his death in 1936. Among his favorite writers were such predecessors as Edgar Allan Poe, Ambrose Bierce, and Arthur Machen. In his letters, he often extolled the talents of his contemporaries in *Weird Tales*, notably H.P. Lovecraft but also including August W. Derleth, Frank Belknap Long, Kirk Mashburn, E. Hoffman Price, Clark Ashton Smith, and Donald Wandrei, several of whom he knew through correspondence.

In the succession of talented authors specializing in the supernatural and macabre, Howard is among the figures from the first decades of the twentieth century who bridge on one hand the older gothic traditions of Poe, Bierce, Machen, J. Sheridan LeFanu, Mary W. Shelley, Bram Stoker, and Edith Wharton, and on the other the modern school that emerged in the post-World War II era and the decades following, including Clive Barker, Charles Beaumont, Ramsey Campbell, Stephen King, Richard Matheson, and Peter Straub.

Myth-making and Eulogy

It's a sad irony that this type of fiction for which Howard had such an affinity, which was largely confined to a relatively small, poorly paying niche market in his time, would burst into a lucrative mainstream category decades after his death with *Rosemary's Baby*, *The Exorcist*, and the bestsellers of Stephen King and Anne Rice. In this respect as in others, Robert E. Howard was a myth-maker ahead of his time. At least we can appreciate the bounty that he left us.

This book is dedicated to the memories of Ted Dikty, Don Grant, Glenn Lord, and Bob Weinberg, whose names frequently appear in the pages that follow, and to the memory of another departed friend and fellow Howard enthusiast, Jim Neal, whose name will be familiar to veteran readers of Marvel Comics' *Savage Sword of Conan*. I trust they would have liked the volume at hand.

For each story, I've included a note indicating where it may be found in current collections of pure-text, carefully curated Howard weird fantasy. A list of those collections, citing publisher and publication date for each, appears at the end of this book.

Cthulhu Mythos

Like other writers of the *Weird Tales* school, including Robert Bloch, August W. Derleth, Henry Kuttner, Frank Belknap Long, Clark Ashton Smith, and Donald Wandrei, Robert E. Howard was a friend and correspondent of H.P. Lovecraft, who is often called the twentieth century's pre-eminent writer of supernatural fiction. Howard and Lovecraft admired each other and carried on a stream of voluminous, sometimes intellectually contentious, but always respectful and affectionate correspondence from 1930 until Howard's death in 1936.

Lovecraft said that Howard was "almost alone in his ability to create real emotions of spectral fear and dread suspense." Howard in turn expressed the opinion that "undoubtedly [Lovecraft] must have the most unusual and wonderfully constructed brain of any man in the world. He alone can paint pictures in shadows and make them terrifically real." Lovecraft's grief over Howard's death is palpable in his letters and in his tribute, "Robert E. Howard: A Memoriam."

Howard was so impressed by Lovecraft's work that he was inspired to write in emulation of his friend, joining Derleth, Long, Smith, and Wandrei as one of the inaugural writers in the development of what has come to be termed Lovecraft's "Cthulhu Mythos." This body of supernatural fantasy is based on the premise that a secret occult lore is contained in ancient texts long suppressed by orthodox religion and science. Those brash or foolish enough to explore this body of legend learn that dreadful entities pre-dating the accepted scientific history of Earth still exist.

With names like Cthulhu, Yog-Sothoth, and Shub-Niggurath, these beings lurk in remote areas of the world, in sunken cities beneath the sea, in the voids of outer space, and in other dimensions contiguous with ours. Worshipped or dreaded as gods by cultists, they are ever ready to re-emerge when the right ceremonies are performed and the right alignments are in place.

This concept became increasingly systematized as time went on, as Bloch, Kuttner, and other younger writers began to contribute, and as Lovecraft in turn incorporated the concepts of Howard and the rest into his own stories. As Howard referred to Lovecraft's Cthulhu, Yog-Sothoth, and Dagon in his tales (the first writer besides Lovecraft himself to do so in print, to my knowledge), Lovecraft cited Howard's *Nameless Cults* as a basic text of the Mythos alongside his own *Necronomicon*. Howard's tome, ascribed to an ill-fated scholar, Von Junzt, was first mentioned in print in "The Children of the Night" (*Weird Tales*, April-May 1931).

In that weird fantasy story (which also formed the cornerstone of Howard's horror cycle about the "Little People," in which context it will be discussed at greater length elsewhere in this book), Howard name-checked Cthulhu, Yog-Sothoth, and Smith's Tsathoggua alongside his own creation Golgoroth, who would re-appear in "The Gods of Bal-Sagoth" in the October 1931 issue of *Weird Tales*.

In the meantime (October 1930), Howard had congratulated his friend on learning that a new Lovecraft story had been accepted by *Weird Tales*. In "The Whisperer in Darkness," published in the August 1931 issue, Lovecraft retrofitted into the expanding Mythos two concepts by Howard, "L'mur-Kathulos" and "Bran." The former was a reference to Howard's character Kathulos from "Skull-Face" (*Weird Tales*, serialized in the October through December 1929 issues). Kathulos was a revivified sorcerer or super-scientist from sunken Atlantis, not Lemuria as "L'mur" might imply. But this sort of apparent inconsistency delights fans of the Mythos, inspiring them to speculate on whys and wherefores.

"Bran" referred to Bran Mak Morn, Howard's hero who led the fading kingdom of the Picts against Roman aggression in ancient Britain. "The Children of the Night" mentioned a secret cult venerating Bran in association with those cults dedicated to Lovecraft's cosmic entities. Later, in "The Shadow Out of

Time" (*Astounding Stories,* June 1936), we read of "the reptile people of fabled Valusia," whom Lovecraft appropriated from Howard's "The Shadow Kingdom" (*Weird Tales*, August 1929).

Howard's signature contribution to the coalescing Mythos was the dreadful volume *Nameless Cults*, his corollary to Lovecraft's "hideous *Necronomicon* of the mad Arab Abdul Alhazred." Of *Nameless Cults*, a character in "The Children of the Night" warns: "There's a book to keep you awake at night!" The imaginary library or "pseudobiblia" of the Mythos is as integral to the cycle of stories as the cosmic entities themselves. Other examples include *De Vermiis Mysteriis* (Robert Bloch), *Cultes des Goules* (August W. Derleth), *Revelations of Glaaki* (Ramsey Campbell), and *Cthaat Aquadingen* (Brian Lumley).

Howard, Lovecraft, and their colleagues often lent an illusion of reality to their forbidden volumes by listing them alongside actual books. In "The Children of the Night," for example, *Nameless Cults* sits on a bookshelf alongside Horace Walpole's *The Castle of Otranto* (1764) and the Marquis de Grosse's *Horrid Mysteries* (1796). For more on the texts of the Mythos, see "H.P. Lovecraft: The Books" by Lin Carter (*The Shuttered Room & Other Pieces*, ed. August Derleth: Arkham House, 1959) and "Books That Never Were" by L. Sprague de Camp (*The Magazine of Fantasy and Science Fiction*, December 1972).

Published in Düsseldorf, Germany, and also known as the "Black Book," *Nameless Cults* was reprinted in a "cheap and faulty translation which was pirated in London by Bridewall in 1845," and then in a "carefully expurgated edition put out by the Golden Goblin Press of New York, 1909." The protagonist of Howard's story "The Black Stone" believes that the original edition is unlikely to exist in "more than half a dozen...volumes in the entire world today." The book is bound in "heavy black leather covers and rusty iron hasps."

Howard reports that the author, Von Junzt, "spent his entire life (1795–1840) delving into forbidden subjects; he traveled in all parts of the world, gained entrance into innumerable secret societies, and read countless little-known and esoteric books and manuscripts in the original; and in the chapters of the Black Book, which range from startling clarity of exposition to murky ambiguity, there are statements and hints to freeze the blood of a thinking man. Reading what Von Junzt *dared* put in print arouses uneasy speculations as to what it was that he dared *not* tell."

Von Junzt was preparing a further manuscript, impliedly containing information withheld from *Nameless Cults*, when he was discovered dead in a locked room, with "the marks of taloned fingers on his throat." The friend who found the corpse, a Frenchman named Alexis Ladeau, on discovering Von Junzt's manuscript lying around the room in fragments, "spent a whole night piecing the fragments together and reading what was written, burnt them to ashes and cut his own throat with a razor."

Some Mythos stories refer to *Nameless Cults* under its putative German title of *Unaussprechlichen Kulten*. That title was suggested by August W. Derleth rather than devised by Howard himself. Howard employed it only once, in an unfinished tale, apparently after Lovecraft informally approved it by referring to the German title in "The Dreams in the Witch-House" (*Weird Tales*, July 1933).

Howard's other substantial addition to the Mythos was the macabre poet Justin Geoffrey, author of the works *Out of the Old Land* and *The People of the Monolith*. Geoffrey "died screaming in a madhouse" after delving too deeply into matters suggested by Von Junzt. In Lovecraft's "The Thing on the Doorstep" (written in 1933, published in *Weird Tales*, January 1937), Justin Geoffrey is a "close correspondent" of Lovecraft's character Edward Pickman Derby, another morbid poet.

In a description that includes some of Howard's own phraseology, Lovecraft refers to Justin Geoffrey as "the notorious Baudelairean poet" who "died screaming in a madhouse in 1926 after a visit to a sinister, ill-regarded village in Hungary." More recently, Brian Lumley and Lin Carter have alluded to Justin Geoffrey in their Cthulhu Mythos stories.

This section of *The Annotated Guide to Robert E. Howard's Weird Fantasy* discusses the five stories that form the core of Howard's contribution to the Cthulhu Mythos, followed by notes regarding other stories that are often classified as "Mythos." For a more detailed analysis of Howard's tales that emulate H.P. Lovecraft's in themes and style, see *Ar-I-E'Ch and the Spell of*

Cthulhu: An Informal Guide to R.E. Howard's Lovecraftian Fiction (Pulp Hero Press, 2018) by the present writer. Although "The Children of the Night" was the first of Howard's published stories to employ and elaborate on Lovecraft's concepts, it more centrally belongs to the Little People cycle. Consequently, it is included and addressed in that section instead.

The Black Stone
First published in *Weird Tales*, November 1931

MAIN CHARACTERS
- Unnamed narrator
- Von Junzt (by reference)
- Justin Geoffrey (by reference)
- Count Boris Vladinoff (by reference)
- Selim Bahadur (by reference)
- Innkeeper
- Innkeeper's nephew
- Schoolmaster
- Cultists of the Black Stone

THE PLOT
The narrator learns of a mysterious relic, the Black Stone, from a reference in Von Junzt's *Nameless Cults*. Von Junzt refers to it cryptically as "one of the keys." A key to what? The narrator investigates further, but what little information he acquires about this ancient monolith in the mountains of Hungary is equally vague. One legend holds that anyone who sleeps near the stone, particularly on Midsummer Night, will go insane.

In Stregoicavar, the village nearest the Black Stone, where Count Boris Vladinoff was killed in an artillery barrage in a battle with Turks in the 1500s while reading a curious account by the Turkish scribe Selim Bahadur, the narrator stays at an inn where the macabre poet Justin Geoffrey had lodged a few years before. Told that Geoffery later died in a madhouse, the innkeeper responds, "Poor lad—he looked too long at the black stone." The narrator's host says that the mountains long ago were inhabited by a brutish people, now extinct, who practiced pagan rites. They lived in a village called Xuthltan, on the site where Stregoicavar now stands.

The narrator finds the Black Stone to be a badly defaced block, carved with remnants of hieroglyphics that remind him of symbols he once saw etched into a stone in Yucatan. Back in the village, the innkeeper's nephew recounts a dream he experienced after sleeping near the stone, in which the monolith appeared as the spire of a massive black castle. On Midsummer Night, returning to the stone, the narrator dreams or witnesses a ritual by skin-clad primitives in which, after flagellation and the sacrifice of an infant, an obscene toad-like creature materializes atop the Black Stone. As a bound girl is offered to the bloated monster, the narrator faints.

Finding the parchment read by the sixteenth-century Count Vladinoff, the narrator learns that it recorded an incident in which the invading Turks had exterminated a tribe of brutish cultists and discovered a cavern in which they slew a toad-like demon "with flame and ancient steel blessed in old times by Muhammad, and with incantations that were old when Arabia was young." With the parchment, he finds a golden idol of a grisly "toad-like being" identical to the creature in his dream. He realizes that in the dream or vision, he had witnessed the ghosts of the slain cultists worshipping their hideous deity. Moreover, he infers that the cavern in which the monster was slain was actually the remnant of the antediluvian black castle of which the innkeeper's nephew had dreamed.

The narrator now knows that the Black Stone is one of the "Keys to Outer Doors" of existence beyond human understanding. The monster of the Black Stone is dead, but clues to other ancient horrors still remain to be rediscovered. "What nameless shapes may even now lurk in the dark places of the world?"

COMMENT

"The Black Stone" is one of Howard's most reprinted stories. An early champion was August W. Derleth, who included it in the 1946 memorial collection of what he considered to be Howard's best work, *Skull-Face & Others*. Derleth also selected it as one of nineteen works "representative of the host written for the Mythos" in his 1969 anthology, *Tales of the Cthulhu Mythos*, alongside other early classics by Frank Belknap Long, Clark Ashton Smith, and Lovecraft. Many fans of a certain age are likely to have encountered it first in one of the mass-market paperbacks reprinted from the hardcover edition of Derleth's book in the early 1970s, or in the Lancer Books collection of several non-series weird fantasies by Howard, *Wolfshead* (1968; second edition, 1972).

The story closely follows the style and construction of Lovecraft's seminal "The Call of Cthulhu," which a character in "The Children of the Night" praises as one of "the three master horror-tales," in the company of Edgar Allan Poe's "The Fall of the House of Usher" and Arthur Machen's "Novel of the Black Seal." Too, in Howard's personal estimation, "it is my honest opinion that these three are the outstanding tales" of the genre, he told Lovecraft.

The setting in mountainous Hungary suggests *Dracula*, which Howard had read. The story of Count Vladinoff reflects his interest in the historical clashes between the East and the West that he began to put to good use around this same time with his work for *Oriental Stories*.

In retrospect, we recognize "The Black Stone" as one of the building-blocks of the developing Mythos. At the time of its publication, a discerning reader of *Weird Tales* would have classified it as an accomplished pastiche of "The Call of Cthulhu." As in Lovecraft's story, a narrator happens upon apparently unrelated or tenuously related fragments of odd information. As he begins to correlate the information piece by piece, he comes to realize that "Man was not always master of the earth." Secret, malicious cults guard hidden knowledge about supernatural entities who once dominated our world. These entities stand ready to return when summoned by formulae either set forth or hinted at in suppressed texts.

In "The Call of Cthulhu," the narrator is drawn to investigate when he finds a grotesque bas-relief figure and other puzzling items left by his recently deceased uncle. The final evidence that correlates the rest and completes the puzzle is a written account by a Scandinavian ship's mate, also now deceased. In "The Black Stone," the narrator becomes curious about cryptic references to the Black Stone in a copy of Von Junzt's book. From other sources, including three further books invented by Howard, a "rat-eaten and mouldering copy" of Dostmann's *Remnants of Lost Empires*, Dornly's *Magyar Folklore*, and Larson's *Turkish Wars*, the narrator gathers additional information. However, it's only when he disinters Selim Bahadur's manuscript and a "squat idol carved of gold" that he succeeds in putting the pieces together.

In Lovecraft's tale, a secret wisdom flows globally, unseen, through different cultures around the world, with its origins in vastly remote ages predating the human race. A voodoo cult in the Louisiana bayous is somehow linked with a secret brotherhood in the mountains of China. A bizarre figurine fashioned by a modern sculptor after a fever dream bears the same outlandish form as an idol captured by police in a raid on a degenerate orgiastic ceremony years before.

In similar fashion, Howard's character finds that the remnants of defaced hieroglyphics on the Black Stone in Hungary suggest characters that he studied on ruins a hemisphere away: "...crude scratches on a gigantic and strangely symmetrical rock in a lost valley of Yucatan." The narrator remembers that in its symmetry, the rock in Yucatan might have been the base of a "long-vanished," consciously designed column, but if so in proportion, such a column would have to have been "a thousand feet high." This detail resonates later when accruing evidence suggests that the narrator's supposition had been correct, however fantastic, once he realizes that the Black Stone is also the remnant of an unimaginably ancient, towering pre-human structure.

The Black Stone, says Howard's narrator, is the merest spire of a "Cyclopean black castle" now buried under the mountains. "Cyclopean" in its meaning of massive stonework structures was one of Lovecraft's favorite adjectives. It stems from usage in the ancient world, when the classic Greeks wondered whether the great masonry ruins of Bronze Age Mycenae had been built by the fabled Cyclops. The term appears in "The Call of Cthulhu" in describing "great Cyclopean cities of titan blocks and sky-flung monoliths" erected by pre-human entities. By employing it in "The Black Stone," Howard further acknowledged his inspiration in Lovecraft's novelette.

Both Lovecraft and Howard suggest that sex orgies are a component of the ceremonies by which their cultists worship Cthulhu and the monster of the Black Stone. In "The Call of Cthulhu," "[a]nimal fury and orgiastic license...[whip] themselves to daemoniac heights by howls and squawking ecstasies" at a clandestine cultists' ritual. "Void of clothing," the cultists surround a monolith on which a statue of Cthulhu rests, and sacrifice kidnapped women and children over a bonfire while "braying, bellowing, and writhing." "[T]he faint beating of great wings, and a glimpse of shining eyes and a mountainous white bulk" in the night suggest that *something* has answered the cultists' incantations before police interrupt the ritual.

Elsewhere in "The Call of Cthulhu," Lovecraft's narrator finds *The Witch-Cult in Western Europe* (1921) by Margaret Alice Murray among the items gathered by his deceased uncle in the uncle's investigation into the Cthulhu cult. Now mostly discredited, Murray's theses were accepted by many scholars of Lovecraft's and Howard's time. Murray surmised that accounts of sexual rites allegedly practiced by "witches" in venerating the Devil actually reflected a survival of primitive fertility ceremonies involving real or symbolic sexual intercourse.

In these rituals, "so-called 'obscene' or 'indecent' dance[s]" were held "for the promotion of fertility among animals and women." Lovecraft rather ingeniously suggests that Murray had gotten her conclusion backwards. Sexual practices assumed to promote fertility were, instead, part of a system designed to venerate Cthulhu and other entities known as the Great Old Ones. These ceremonies promised a world "free and wild and beyond good and evil, with laws and morals thrown aside," when the Great Old Ones returned.

In "The Black Stone," Howard alludes to Murray's theory when a subsidiary character proposes that the Black Stone was worshipped by a "fertility cult which...gave rise to the tales of witchcraft." The rites practiced in the ceremony dreamed or witnessed by Howard's narrator follow along the same lines as Lovecraft's, but the linkage with fertility traditions is stronger and the sexual elements are more explicit.

The ghostly cultists of the Black Stone react in "slobbering ecstasy" as a naked young woman executes a "bestial and obscene" dance while being flogged by a high priest or shaman in animal skins. Finally, "quivering and panting," the young woman embraces the Black Stone with "fierce hot kisses," as the other worshippers tear off each other's clothing while the priest sacrifices an infant.

Where the pedestal in Lovecraft's ritual hosted only a statue of Cthulhu, a living entity in "The Black Stone" materializes on top of the monolith. It is a "bloated, repulsive" creature, "toad-like," that "suck[s] in its breath, lustfully and slobberingly" as the priest offers the naked woman as a sacrifice. Rather than witness what happens next, Howard's narrator passes out, in much the same way as the protagonists of Lovecraft's stories usually flee or faint when confronted by horrible things. The reader is left to surmise that the creature is a predecessor of Thog in the later Conan adventure "Xuthal of the Dusk" (*Weird Tales*, September 1933, as "The Slithering Shadow")—characterized by the late Fritz Leiber as "an amorphous and ravening Lovecraftian monster with the addition of a unlikely sexual hunger."

Available in *The Horror Stories of Robert E. Howard*

The Thing on the Roof

First published in *Weird Tales*, February 1932

MAIN CHARACTERS

- Unnamed narrator
- Tussmann
- Tussmann's servant
- Von Junzt (by reference)
- Professor James Clement (by reference)

THE PLOT

The narrator, an anthropologist, locates a copy of *Nameless Cults* at the request of his rival, Tussmann. In return, Tussmann promises to retract and apologize for criticism leveled at the narrator three years before in a scientific journal. From Von Junzt's book, Tussmann learns that in an ancient temple in the Honduran jungles, the Temple of the Toad, rests the mummy of a high priest from a forgotten race. A toad-shaped jewel hangs from the mummy's neck, a "key" to a treasure in a crypt underneath.

Tussmann ventures to Honduras, returning to his English estate months later. Invited to Tussmann's home, the narrator finds the grounds badly neglected and hears a large, hoofed animal blundering around in the bushes. Admitted to the house, the narrator finds Tussmann tense and restless. The other man says he found the mummy and the toad-shaped jewel described by Von Junzt. Shown the gem, the narrator finds it "peculiarly repulsive." But in the crypt was "nothing that I could bring away," Tussmann reports.

As Tussmann reads a warning in *Nameless Cults* that "sleeping things" should not be disturbed, a noise comes from upstairs "like a horse stamping around on the roof." The explorer retreats to his room, leaving the narrator to read in *Nameless Cults* about a "huge, tittering, tentacled, hoofed monstrosity" worshipped by the civilization that built the Temple of the Toad. The narrator realizes that the jewel was the "key" to releasing the monster. Chilled by a sudden scream, he rushes into Tussmann's room to find the window-sill smeared with slime and the air foul with a terrible stench. The toad-jewel is missing and Tussmann lies dead on the floor, his head crushed under the "print of an enormous hoof."

COMMENT

"When a writer specifically describes the object of his horror, gives it worldly dimensions and solid shape, he robs it of half its terrors," Howard once remarked to H.P. Lovecraft. "The Thing on the Roof" appears to be his effort to put this precept fully into practice.

The creature in "The Black Stone" was glimpsed briefly. In "The Thing on the Roof," the entity of the title isn't shown at all. Its presence is revealed by incidental details. Before crashing into Tussmann's room, the narrator hears "a hideous high-pitched tittering and then [a] disgusting squashy sound as if a great, jelly-like bulk was being forced through the window," and then "a faint swish of gigantic wings."

Once in the room, he's greeted by a "foul and overpowering stench [that] billowed out like a yellow fog" (recalling Lovecraft's quotation from the *Necronomicon*, that of the Old Ones "[a]s a foulness shall ye know Them"). On the window sill is a smear of "foul, unspeakable slime." These details of stench and slime, the sound of "tittering" as an unpleasant mode of laughter, and the apparent inconsistency in the impression of a "great, jelly-like" entity with hooves and the ability to fly, build a reasonably unsettling picture in the reader's imagination.

The suggestion that the creature is winged and has a gelatinous physical structure mirrors Lovecraft's description of Cthulhu in "The Call of Cthulhu." The sound of hooves like a "horse stamping around" suggests another Lovecraft story, "The Dunwich Horror," as the editor and writer Robert M. Price has suggested. In "The Dunwich Horror," which Howard also esteemed, a character hears what seems to be "a horse stamping" on the second-story floor of the Whateley farmhouse; from later events in the story, it seems that the stamping was made by a creature sired by a Great Old One, Yog-Sothoth, from a human mother.

A few more details emerge about *Nameless Cults*. From an intermediary, Professor James Clement of Richmond, Virginia (probably not coincidentally, one of Edgar Allan Poe's cities of residence), the narrator obtains a copy of the original edition for Tussmann, a "thick, dusty volume with...heavy leather covers and rusty iron hasps," its pages "time-yellowed." Is this the same copy that the narrator in "The Black Stone" consulted, or another copy of this rare printing? Is Professor James Clement the same "Clemants" who appeared in "The Children of the Night," which is surveyed in the next section of this guide? Howard leaves those questions open to conjecture.

We learn that the 1909 edition from Golden Goblin Press "was handsomely bound and decorated with the exquisite and weirdly imaginative illustrations of Diego Vasquez." However, reflecting an earlier reference in "The Black Stone," the text "was so carefully expurgated that fully a fourth of the original matter was cut out," leaving it frustratingly insufficient for Tussmann's purposes in learning more about the mummy in the ruined Central American temple, and the treasure that it supposedly guards. The faulty Bridewell translation is equally poor, mistakenly locating the Temple of the Toad in Guatemala rather than Honduras.

We also learn that Von Junzt "was actually in Honduras" at one time, drawing his information about the temple from first-hand observation. This aspect of "The Thing on the Roof" recalls the passage from "The Black Stone" in which the inscriptions on the Black Stone remind the narrator of markings on a "strangely symmetrical rock in a lost valley of Yucatan." There, only a tenuous association is drawn between the cult of the Black Stone in Hungary and evidence for the existence of the same orthodoxy in South America. "I will not say that the characters on the Black Stone were similar to those on the colossal rock in Yucatan; but one suggested the other," said the narrator of "The Black Stone." He either overlooked or forgot Von Junzt's materials about Central America in *Nameless Cults*, it seems.

Justin Geoffrey appears indirectly with a quote from *Out of the Old Land* as an epigram which alludes to entities that "lift colossal wings / On the high gable roofs / Which tremble to the trample of their mastodonic hoofs."

Howard appears to have written "The Thing on the Roof" late in 1930, according to the invaluable timeline of Howard's fiction at the Howard Works web site. In August 1931, Howard commented to his friend Tevis Clyde Smith that Farnsworth Wright, the editor of *Weird Tales*, rejected the story "[s]everal months ago." The tale "seemed too erudite for the general reader, though he liked it himself," Howard said of Wright's reason for returning the tale. "Claytons likewise rejected it, saying the plot was too thin etc." "Claytons" was Clayton Magazines, publisher of *Strange Tales*, a *Weird Tales* competitor.

On the next try, "*Argosy* rejected it with the usual stereotype" or form letter. And then Farnsworth Wright "asked to see it again" and this time accepted it, paying Howard $40. Given the magazine's policy of paying on publication and not acceptance, Howard probably didn't see a check until after the tale appeared in the August 1932 *Weird Tales*. This is assuming that the story wasn't among those for which *Weird Tales* owed Howard $800 in back payment as of May 1935.

Howard thought highly of "The Thing on the Roof," which he lauded as "not only the best story by far that I ever wrote, but which is, in my honest opinion a really first-class weird story judged by any standards." Howard's enthusiasm may have been based, in part, on his relief in finally placing it for publication. "I'd have given it to [Wright] free, just to get it in print," he told his friend Tevis Clyde Smith. In a letter two years later, he told August W. Derleth that "The Black Stone" and "other kindred yarns of mine" were "written more as experiments than anything else, and I soon saw that they were not my natural style."

Howard never abandoned the Lovecraft influence altogether, but his other three core stories in the Mythos depart from the style of "The Black Stone" and "The Thing on the Roof," in which a narrator assembles a mosaic of information from disparate sources much like the protagonist of "The Call of Cthulhu." The other three stories place their protagonists at the unfolding center of the action; two were salvaged by Howard from earlier manuscripts outside the Mythos, and two of the three combine the Mythos with Howard's bent for fast action.

Available in *The Horror Stories of Robert E. Howard*

The Fire of Asshurbanipal

First published in *Weird Tales*, December 1936

MAIN CHARACTERS

- Steve Clarney
- Yar Ali
- Nureddin El Mekru
- Elderly Bedouin
- One-eyed Bedouin
- Nureddin's thieves
- Xuthltan the sorcerer (by reference)

THE PLOT

Steve Clarney, an American, and his partner, Yar Ali, an Afghan, are left afoot in the Arabian desert after a sandstorm, and then attacked by Bedouin raiders. Repelling the assault with rifle fire, they continue on in their quest to find the lost city of Kara-Shehr, designated as the City of Evil in the *Necronomicon*. They hope to discover a fabled gem, the Fire of Asshurbanipal, said to be clutched by the skeleton of a long-dead sultan.

The next day they find the ancient city, its throne room, and the blazing jewel as promised (or warned) by the *Necronomicon*, but they're interrupted by the main body of Bedouins whose scouts they tangled with the day before. The leader of the thieves is Nureddin El Mekru, an old enemy of Clarney's. Nureddin determines to put Steve and Yar Ali to death, but first, mesmerized by the Fire of Asshurbanipal, he decides to claim it from the clasp of the skeleton that holds it. An elderly Arab in the gang entreats him not to take the jewel, saying that it was cursed by a magician named Xuthltan. A demon guards the Fire and will destroy anyone who tries to take it.

Unfazed, the raider grabs the gem, which seems to emit "a sharp inhuman cry," and a hidden door opens, from which a tentacle seizes Nureddin and draws him into the opening. After the other Bedouins flee in terror, the door opens again. "Monstrous eyes" glow in the darkness. Steve and Yar Ali close their eyes as "a horrific evil too grisly for human comprehension...an Invader from Outer Gulfs" enters the throne room. The creature places the jewel back in the skeleton's hand and leaves the severed head of Nureddin on the dais of the throne. "God help us," says Clarney, who caught one glimpse of the entity as it returned to its hiding place, "it was the monster that Xuthltan called up out of the dark blind caverns of the earth to guard the Fire of Asshurbanipal!"

COMMENT

Talbot Mundy and H.P. Lovecraft were two of Howard's favorite authors. Mundy is best if faintly remembered today for *King of the Khyber Rifles* (1916), filmed by John Ford in a very loose adaptation as *The Black Watch* (1929), remade even more loosely under Mundy's original title as a Tyrone Power film in 1957, and adapted in comic book form by Classics Illustrated. In his early stories for *Adventure* magazine in the 1920s, Mundy created Jimgrim, a freelance peacekeeper in British-administered Jerusalem and Palestine who bumps up against Bedouin raiders in *The Lion of Petra* (1922) and other novels. Had Mundy and Lovecraft ever established an unlikely partnership, "The Fire of Asshurbanipal" would have been the result.

"The Fire of Asshurbanipal" begins as an adventure in the Middle East in the manner of Howard's swashbuckling yarns about Francis X. Gordon (El Borak), which were finally collected in hardcover book form in the 1970s by Ted Dikty and Darrell Richardson for FAX Collector's Editions. Then the story audaciously concludes on a Lovecraftian note of cosmic terror. In an earlier version of the story, the elements of the Cthulhu Mythos were absent except for a passing reference to the *Necronomicon*. In that version, Nureddin is killed by an adder as he reaches for the accursed jewel, and Steve and Yar Ali appropriate the jewel after the outlaw gang flees. In that form, "The Fire of Asshurbanipal" appears in the collection *El Borak and Other Desert Adventures* (Ballantine Books/Del Rey, 2010).

In revising the story as a weird fantasy, Howard added the character of the elderly Bedouin who warns Nureddin not to take the jewel, the backstory of Xuthltan and his curse, and references to "Cthulhu and Koth and Yog-Sothoth, and all the pre-Adamite Dwellers in the black cities under the sea and the caverns of the earth."

The transition from gun-blazing action to intimations of cosmic horror begins as the two heroes enter the City of Evil:

> They came to the portals of the great temple. Rows of immense columns flanked the wide doorway, which was ankle-deep in sand, and from which sagged massive bronze frameworks that had once braced mighty doors, whose polished woodwork had rotted away centuries ago. They passed into a mighty hall of misty twilight whose shadowy stone roof was upheld by columns like the trunks of forest trees. The whole effect of the architecture was one of awesome magnitude and sullen, breathtaking splendor, like a temple built by somber giants for the abode of dark gods.

The atmosphere of mystery extends to the disclosure of the Fire of Asshurbanipal, which "throbs and pulses like the heart of a cobra," as if organic rather than crystalline. In the earlier, non-fantastic version of the story, it appeared more prosaically as "a great ruby, as big as a pigeon's egg."

The monster is described by Clarney from a brief glimpse: "It was gigantic and black and shadowy; it was a hulking monstrosity that walked upright like a man, but it was like a toad, too, and it was winged and tentacled. I saw only its back; if I'd seen the front of it—its face—I'd have undoubtedly lost my mind." Although a fearless man of action, Clarney also exhibits the behavior of a typical Lovecraft protagonist when confronted by a dreadful creature of the Mythos—"he fainted for the only time in his chequered life."

Xuthltan, a name that appears in "The Black Stone" to designate an ancient pagan village, here becomes the name of a wizard, a practitioner of "black wisdom," in ancient Babylon. Howard sometimes, as here, used names over and over again in different and often contradictory contexts. With the hope but little likelihood that his stories would survive beyond one-shot appearances in transitory pulp magazines, Howard would not have worried over such conundrums. Today, such details are grist for readers who may delight in inferring their own associations between Xuthltan the village and Xuthltan the magician, or for that matter Xaltotun, a similar name bestowed upon a different sorcerer in the Conan novel *The Hour of the Dragon*.

Fans who esteem Howard's sword-and-sorcery are likely to rate "The Fire of Asshurbanipal" at the top of his Mythos tales for its merging of action and horror. On its original *Weird Tales* appearance, it earned a beautiful cover painting by J. Allen St. John, best remembered now as the premier illustrator of cover jackets for Edgar Rice Burroughs' adventure novels in the 1920s and '30s.

Available in *The Horror Stories of Robert E. Howard*

Dig Me No Grave

First published in *Weird Tales*, February 1937

MAIN CHARACTERS

- Kirowan
- John Conrad
- John Grimlan
- A stranger from Asia

THE PLOT

Kirowan is awakened in the dead of night by his friend John Conrad, who requests his company in walking to the "great dark house" of the reclusive John Grimlan. Grimlan has just died, and Conrad asks for Kirowan's help in carrying out Grimlan's instructions for the disposition of his body. Grimlan was a scholar and traveler to remote places, "universally detested and feared" for his evil disposition. "[T]he country people always claimed that in his youth [Grimlan] sold his soul to the Devil."

Grimlan had died in great, convulsive agony, apparently more emotional than physical. In the twenty years that Kirowan knew him, he had never seemed to age, always appearing as a man of about fifty. In his will, Grimlan had asked that his estate be left to an Asian, Malik Tous—a name which Kirowan recognizes as that of "the foul god worshipped by the mysterious Yezidees."

In Grimlan's house, the two men read the recluse's injunction: "Dig me no grave; I shall not need one." They also study a parchment listing the name of "John Grymlann, borne, March 10, 1630. Died March 10, 1930"—that very day's date. Beneath is a seal in the shape of a peacock, the sign of Malik Tous. Upstairs, they encounter a man of Asian appearance who has already executed some of Grimlan's instructions by covering the corpse with a robe that bears an ambiguous figure of a peacock, bat, or dragon, and lighting seven black candles around the body. "[H]ow had he come to the Grimlan house so quickly?"

Conrad reads Grimlan's instructions aloud, which refer in archaic language to "ye black citadels of Koth &...ye Darke Lord whose face is hidden," from whom one "for a price may...gain hys heartes desire, ryches & knowldege beyond countinge." As Conrad's recital proceeds, the candles begin to go out one by one. Kirowan dreads that "some nameless, abominable thing" will occur when the last flame dies. A groan resounds through the room, apparently from under the robe that covers the dead man. The last candle goes out, and darkness falls with a rush of wind and "an intolerable odor."

Conrad re-lights a candle. The mysterious Asian is gone, as is Grimlan's corpse. Kirowan and Conrad flee the house, looking back as flames engulf it. "Soul and body [Grimlan] sold to Malik Tous, who is Satan, two hundred and fifty years ago," Conrad cries. From the smoke and flames, a gigantic, bat-shaped shadow rises, clutching "a small white thing" with the appearance of a corpse. "The Fiend has claimed his own!"

COMMENT

"Dig Me No Grave" was another rewrite. The late Glenn Lord reported that it was originally a non-Mythos story, "John Grimlan's Debt," that Howard unsuccessfully submitted to *Ghost Stories* magazine, where he had placed one tale, "The Spirit of Tom Molyneaux," published as "The Apparition in the Prize Ring." Rewritten as "Dig Me No Grave" to incorporate Mythos elements, it was one of three manuscripts (another was the Mythos version of "The Fire of Asshurbanipal") placed with *Weird Tales* after Howard's death.

The Mythos elements of the story exist in a teasingly odd way with the pre-existing references to Malik Tous and the Yezidees. In Howard's time, most Americans probably knew of the Yezidees only through sensational fiction like Robert W. Chambers' 1920 novel *The Slayer of Souls*, where they are conflated with the Muslim sect of the Assassins as sinister diabolists who scheme with "Anarchists, terrorists, Bolshevists, [and] Reds of all shades and degrees" to conquer the West after World War I. There was a copy of Chambers' novel in Howard's library.

Where Chambers' Yezidees worship the evil Central Asian god Erlik, Howard may have grafted on Malik Tous from references in the fiction of his friend, E. Hoffman Price, saving Erlik for other stories and for the background of his Conan stories, where he is one of the Hyborian Age gods. In "Dig Me No Grave," Howard's conceit traces all evil back to a common source, the "Black Master," or the "Darke Lord," regarded as Malik Tous by Muslims and identified by other faiths as "the Prince of Darkness—Ahriman—the old Serpent—the veritable Satan!"

Of the Mythos references, Conrad remembers a question by Grimlan, "What do you know of Yog-Sothoth, of Kathulos and the sunken cities?...Not even in your dreams have you glimpsed the black cyclopean walls of Koth, or shriveled before the noxious winds that blow from Yuggoth!" In the parchment read by Conrad, Grimlan speaks of "ye black citadels of Koth" inhabited by "ye Darke Lord whose face is hidden," and of "ye dedde citie of Koth." The planet Yuggoth was mentioned in Lovecraft's sonnet-cycle "Fungi from Yuggoth" and in "The Whisperer in Darkness." In "The Case of Charles Dexter Ward," written in 1927 but not published until 1943, Lovecraft writes of "the sign of Koth, that dreamers see fixed above the archway of a certain black tower standing alone in twilight."

How or whether Lovecraft's Koth relates (or not) to Howard's is open for debate, as is the question of how or whether Koth as a city in "Dig Me No Grave" relates (or not) to the allusion in "The Fire of Asshurbanipal," which seems to identify Koth as an entity like Cthulhu and Yog-Sothoth. The phrase "Kathulos and the sunken cities" doubles back on Lovecraft's incorporation of Kathulos, "Skull-Face," into the Mythos in "The Whisperer in Darkness."

"Before Manne ye Elder ones were, & even yet their lord dwelleth among ye shadows...," runs another line in Grimlan's testament. The sentence simultaneously affirms the story's association with the Mythos and suggests that the "Black Master" himself is an incarnation or avatar of an Elder or Great Old One. Had Howard written more Mythos stories, he might have returned to the "Black Master" and associated him with Lovecraft's Nyarlathotep, "a deputy or messenger of hidden and terrible powers—the 'Black Man' of the witch-cult."

Characters named "Kirowan" and "Conrad" appear in several of Howard's weird fantasies, and some readers assume that all of those characters named "Conrad" are the same person, and likewise all the "Kirowans." Whether this is the case is open to discussion. Howard tended to use certain names over and over again with no intent to associate one usage with another. "Costigan," "Allison," and "Brill" are examples. Some who infer a "Kirowan and Conrad" series speculate that these stories might have represented Howard's attempt at an "occult detective" sequence similar to Seabury Quinn's popular thrillers about Jules de Grandin in *Weird Tales,* or Sax Rohmer's Paul Harley tales. More on this issue in the "Psychic Investigators" section later in this guide.

Available in The Horror Stories of Robert E. Howard

The Hoofed Thing

First published as "Usurp the Night" in *Weirdbook* No. 3, 1970

MAIN CHARACTERS

- Michael Strang
- Marjory Ash
- John Stark
- Marjory's mother
- Townspeople

THE PLOT

Cats are disappearing from the streets of an unnamed small town or suburb. Michael Strang investigates when his sweetheart Marjory's Maltese vanishes. In canvassing the neighborhood, he meets a newcomer, John Stark, a powerfully built recluse with a physical impairment. The two men discover they have a common interest in esoteric studies. While in Stark's old house, Strang hears what appears to be the scampering of a small hoofed animal, upstairs. More pets disappear, dogs this time, and Marjory's new bulldog Bozo is nearly one. And then children begin to vanish, and then a homeless person. On further visits to Stark's house, Michael hears more sounds from upstairs, growing louder each time.

In his copy of Von Junzt's *Nameless Cults* in the "rare Düsseldorf edition" with "its iron-clasped leather bindings," Michael reads of creatures summoned from other dimensions to "feast on the blood of men." Dozing, he dreams that Marjory is calling for him. Bozo appears at his door, battered and bloody, and Strang follows him to Stark's house, where he finds Marjory tied up and hears "gargantuan hoofs blundering to and fro" upstairs. The noise is made by a "thing from out the Abyss" that was small when first conjured by Stark, then grew larger on blood from animals and then humans supplied by him, and now has reached full size. Michael finds the recluse dead, slain by the creature. Attacked by "the Horror," Strang slashes it to pieces with a broadsword. As the thing's tissues melt into a still-living black pool "showing a million facets and gleams of light," Michael sets fire to the house and flees with Marjory and Bozo.

COMMENT

Howard had mixed success in selling to *Strange Tales*, full title *Strange Tales of Mystery and Terror*, a rival to *Weird Tales* that ran from 1931 to 1933. The magazine bought three of his stories but rejected at least two others, including "The Hoofed Thing." Learning of the publication's impending demise (which left one of the purchased stories unpaid-for and unpublished), Howard said in 1932 that he "wasn't surprized. *Strange Tales* was too narrow in policy to have lasted long."

It isn't clear what Howard meant, but he may have been referring to the fact that the magazine appeared to favor stories with modern, often mundane settings and a relatively brisk narrative pace. With its setting in an ordinary neighborhood where John Stark's "rundown, rambling estate" is an anomaly, "The Hoofed Thing" could hardly be more contemporary in externals. Perhaps the editor was put off by the Mythos elements, although Clark Ashton Smith's story "The Nameless Offspring" in the June 1932 issue could be regarded as a Mythos story, opening as it does with a "quotation" from the *Necronomicon*.

In perusing *Nameless Cults*, Strang remarks upon "the deep and sinister wisdom behind [Von Junzt's] incredible assertions as I read of the unseen worlds of unholy dimensions which... press, horrific and dimly guessed, on our universe." This appears to suggest a greater clarity in Von Junzt's text than indicated by "The Black Stone" and "The Thing on the Roof," where the meaning of the term "keys" eluded the protagonists until all the evidence fell into place.

Or the sticking point for *Strange Tales* may not have been the Mythos content, but instead the tale's apparent dissonance in tone, as the apparently mild-mannered Michael Strang suddenly snatches up a broadsword handed down from "a Crusading ancestor" to do battle with the creature conjured by Stark. If so, most Howard fans would probably beg to differ. The novelty of a protagonist physically engaging with the monster, instead of fainting or running, adds a unique aspect to the Mythos formula. Strang even appears to rival Conan for strength and tenacity, enduring the pain of a broken arm while swinging the ponderous sword with his one good hand, shearing "straight through the pulpy unstable bulk" of Stark's monster.

Heralded by the stamping of its hooves, like the entity in "The Thing on the Roof," Stark's creature is described in full: "Twice as tall as a man, the general outline was not unlike that of a human; but its gigantic legs terminated in huge hoofs and instead of arms, a dozen tentacles writhed like snakes about its huge bloated torso. Its color was a leprous, mottled reptilian hue...its sparkling million-faceted eyes...glittered like bits of fire." The hoofs are carried over from "The Thing on the Roof."

By bringing the monster into full view, Howard may have decided that he was better off rethinking his belief that explicitly depicting a horrific figure "robs it of half its terrors," and instead indulging his penchant for physical action. When the thing's fragments "*melt* into a viscous black stenching fluid" after Strang plies his sword, still alive after dismemberment, the reader may remember the scene in "The Call of Cthulhu" in which Cthulhu's "scattered plasticity" begins to re-form after the entity is smashed apart by the bow of a ship.

The story follows the traditional Mythos pattern in assembling a series of clues that lead to an eventual revelation. Strang seems slow on the uptake, even for a Mythos character who is required by the traditional formula to remain oblivious until all of the clues come together. Even after Stark is barely foiled in an apparent attempt to knock Strang out or kill him with a mallet, his reflected face "hideously distorted," Strang is undecided. Is the recluse a madman, perhaps responsible for the disappearances in the neighborhood? Or: "Had I let my imagination run away with me?" He even thinks to "go back to Mr. Stark's house and apologize" for his suspicions.

Strang decides that Stark could not have perpetrated the murders because he has a physical impairment, a seemingly misshapen foot that would hinder the speed and stealth of a nocturnal kidnapper. Besides, why would a "refined, elderly scholar" engage in abduction and murder? The plot illustrates the difficulties in unrolling a series of events that will keep the reader guessing, while adequately laying reasonable groundwork for the final outcome. If you're a Howard or Mythos fan, you're probably inclined to go along for the ride.

Available in *The Horror Stories of Robert E. Howard*

Notes

- In addition to inclusion in *The Horror Stories of Robert E. Howard*, Howard's Mythos fiction appears in *Nameless Cults: The Cthulhu Mythos Fiction of Robert E. Howard*, edited by Robert M. Price (Chaosium Books, 2001). This volume incorporates both the core works surveyed in this section, and the stories often discussed as Mythos stories because of aspects related to the Mythos: "Skull-Face," "The Shadow Kingdom," "The Little People," "The Gods of Bal-Sagoth," "Black John's Vengeance" (as "The Black Bear Bites"), "The Children of the Night," "The People of the Dark," "Worms of the Earth," and "The Challenge from Beyond." Also collected there are tales by other writers that complete several unfinished Howard works.

- A Mythos story titled "The House" was left unfinished by Howard. Two characters, Kirowan and Conrad (who may or may not be the same duo from "Dig Me No Grave"), set out to discover why the "half-genius, half-maniac" Justin Geoffrey developed a fascination for the outré. The quest leads to an old house in upstate New York. Geoffrey began to suffer vivid nightmares as a boy after spending the night in a circle of oaks around the house. The unfinished story includes two verses by Geoffrey that do not appear in Howard's other Mythos tales. Excerpted by Howard, one of the verses was published as "Arkham" in the August 1932 issue of *Weird Tales*, and the other as "An Open Window" in the September 1932 issue. "The House" was completed by August W. Derleth and published in 1971 as "The House in the Oaks" in an Arkham House anthology, *Dark Things*. In that form, it also appears in the Chaosium book *Nameless Cults*. The original fragment appears in *The Horror Stories of Robert E. Howard*.

- A fragment by Howard begins "Beneath the glare of the sun..." It was first published in *The Howard Collector* No. 9, 1967. Brill, an archaeologist, believes that a newly unearthed dome in a Middle Eastern desert dates from ancient Stygia, a nation in the legendary Hyborian Age of prehistory. He draws that conclusion from a reference in *Nameless Cults* or *Unaussprechlichen Kulten* by "a crazy German named Von Junzt." The fragment is notable for Howard's only use of the German title devised by August W. Derleth. It is also notable for associating the Cthulhu Mythos via Von Junzt's book with the Conan series. Robert M. Price completed the story under the title "Black Eons," in the Chaosium book *Nameless Cults*. The original fragment appears in *The Horror Stories of Robert E. Howard*.

- A fragment, "Dagon Manor," may have been intended by Howard as a Mythos story. "Dagon" appears in Lovecraft's "Dagon" and in "The Shadow over Innsmouth" as a Mythos entity. Based on internal similarities, some Howard students speculate that the fragment represented an initial start on "The Children of the Night." The fragment appears in *Pictures in the Fire*. A version completed by C.J. Henderson appeared in *Shudder Stories* #4, 1986.

- "Worms of the Earth" (*Weird Tales*, November 1932) includes Lovecraftian references to the "[b]lack gods of R'lyeh," "Dagon-moor," and "Dagon's Barrow." R'lyeh is the sunken city in which Cthulhu is imprisoned in "The Call of Cthulhu." "Worms of the Earth" is frequently listed as a Mythos tale because of those allusions, but in substance it is more centrally related to the Little People series discussed below, and even more so to the Bran Mak Morn series, the context in which Bob Weinberg addressed it in *The Annotated Guide to Robert E. Howard's Sword & Sorcery*. As part of the Bran cycle, it was collected in several books, including *Worms of the Earth* (Donald M. Grant, 1974), the first hardcover collection of all the Bran stories. It appears in *Bran Mak Morn: The Last King*.

- "Black John's Vengeance," also published as "The Black Bear Bites," alludes to an "evilly old" cult in Mongolia that worships the Old Ones and "the great Cthulhu." The reference is drawn from Lovecraft's allusion to "undying leaders of the [Cthulhu] cult in the mountains of China," in "The Call of Cthulhu." The Howard story contains no overtly supernatural elements. It is available in *Tales of Weird Menace*.

- "The Challenge from Beyond" is a collaborative story with chapters by C.L. Moore, A. Merritt, H.P. Lovecraft, Robert E. Howard, and Frank Belknap Long. It is routinely classified as a Mythos story because Lovecraft's chapter refers to the "Eltdown Shards," a Mythos text. Howard's section contains no overt Mythos elements. It is surveyed later in the section of this guide on Howard's science fiction.

The Little People

Inspired by the fiction of Arthur Machen (1863–1947), Robert E. Howard wrote a cycle of weird fantasies centering on the proposition that a civilization of small, primitive people preceded the Celts into the British Isles in prehistoric times. Initially, Howard called these people "Picts." In an early tale, "The Lost Race" (*Weird Tales*, December 1927), they were presented sympathetically as having "once ruled Britain from sea to sea" before the invading Celts arrived and drove them into hiding.

Captured by a cave-dwelling tribe of dark, diminutive folk, "[s]carce above four feet" in height, a warrior Briton of the Bronze Age is amazed to learn that they are Picts:

> Tales of their doings, their hatred of the race of man, and their maliciousness flocked back to him. Little he knew that he was gazing on one of the mysteries of the ages. That the tales which the ancient Gaels told of the Picts, already warped, would become even more warped from age to age, to result in tales of elves, dwarfs, trolls and fairies, at first accepted and then rejected, entire, by the race of men, just as the Neanderthal monsters resulted in tales of goblins and ogres.

In "The Little People," a later story, a modern character refers to Machen and a tradition of primitive people "known variously as Turanians, Picts, Mediterraneans, and Garlic-eaters." From Machen came the term "the Little People" and the fancy that the designation "represent[s] a tradition of the prehistoric Turanian inhabitants of the country [that is, the British isles], who were cave dwellers." Machen's novelette "The Shining Pyramid," in which these references occur, is cited by Howard's protagonist, Costigan—not to be confused with Sailor Steve Costigan of Howard's boxing stories, or any of the other "Costigans" with whom Howard's fiction is populated.

Machen's term "Turanian," subsequently adopted by Howard, referred to a now-outdated theory that Europe in the Stone Age was inhabited by a folk of mixed Caucasian and Asian culture and language. "The Little People" follows Machen's lead in imagining that the malicious remnant of these folk survive in out-of-the-way corners of the British Isles as stealthy predators with "stunted bodies,...gnarled limbs,...snake-like, beady eyes." The story was unpublished during Howard's lifetime.

As Howard began to correspond with H.P. Lovecraft in 1930, the two writers exchanged remarks on Machen's fiction and the tradition of the Little People. Howard modified his earlier conception of the Little People. "I readily see the truth of your remarks that a Mongoloid race must have been responsible for the myths of the Little People," he told Lovecraft. At that point he began to differentiate the Picts, fictionally, from "a Mongoloid type, very low in the scale of development," who existed contemporaneously with the Picts in prehistoric Britain.

In "The Children of the Night" (*Weird Tales*, April/May 1931), a character, Conrad, corrects a misconception by Von Juntz in *Nameless Cults*—or perhaps a misinterpretation of Von Junzt by another character, Taverel—that the Picts were of the same debased culture who "gave rise to the tales of earth spirits and goblins." In the ensuing discussion, Conrad argues that "there was nothing about the Picts to excite such horror and repulsion."

Stimulated by Machen and Lovecraft, Howard proceeded to write further about the Little People. This cycle of stories includes "The Little People," "The Children of the Night," "People of the Dark," and "Worms of the Earth." A thematically related tale, "The Valley of the Lost," transposed the basic concept to the American Southwest. Four of the stories are discussed below in the order of publication. "Worms of the Earth," which belongs more centrally to Howard's series about the Pictish king Bran Mak Morn, is surveyed by a brief note at the end of this section.

The Children of the Night

First published in *Weird Tales*, April-May 1931

MAIN CHARACTERS

- John O'Donnel / Aryara
- Ketrick
- Conrad
- Clemants
- Professor Kirowan
- Taverel
- The Children of the Night

THE PLOT

Six enthusiasts of anthropology gather in Conrad's study to discuss esoteric matters. The conversation presently turns to Von Junzt's *Nameless Cults* and its allusions to a modern cult awaiting the return of Bran Mak Morn, the olden Pictish king. Conrad disputes a suggestion that the Picts were the race that "gave rise to the tales of earth spirits and goblins." Instead, he maintains that the latter culture was "a Mongoloid type, very low in the scale of development" and "of extremely inhuman aspect."

As the guests examine a curious, diminutive flint mallet that Conrad displays, one of them, Ketrick, swings the implement, which strikes the narrator, O'Donnel, rendering him unconscious. O'Donnel relives the final moments in his past life as a tribesman named Aryara in ancient Britain. Because of his neglect in dozing off while on sentry duty, the stunted troglodytes known as the Children of the Night have ambushed Aryara's hunting party and butchered his friends in their sleep. Vengefully, Aryara seeks out the predators' village and enacts revenge in "one red sacrifice" to his tribal god Il-marinen. As his bronze axe wreaks havoc, he is overwhelmed by his "leering" foes and killed.

Recovering consciousness, O'Donnel realizes that one of his associates, Ketrick, with his "lisping, hissing voice," bears the "snaky taint" of the Children of the Night. He surmises that a Ketrick ancestress was raped by one of the creatures in times past, and as a result, the DNA of the species was passed down through succeeding generations. To expiate his guilt as Aryara millennia ago in betraying the trust of his friends, he realizes that he must slay Ketrick. Only then "I will have kept faith with my tribe."

COMMENT

Howard's amateur interest in the history, anthropology, and languages of the British Isles was already evident in his letters to friends in the late 1920s. He expressed the same enthusiasm in a 1930 letter to Farnsworth Wright, the editor of *Weird Tales*, in praising H.P. Lovecraft's horror story "The Rats in the Walls," and commenting on linguistic matters suggested by the tale. Forwarded by Wright to Lovecraft, the letter resulted in a long correspondence between Howard and Lovecraft himself.

The early exchanges between the two writers kindled Howard's interest in emulating Lovecraft's Cthulhu Mythos tales, as surveyed in the previous section of this book. The exchanges also generated discussions about early cultures in Europe and the Middle East. Both writers subscribed to the theory that the dominant genetic and cultural strain throughout history was represented by a fair-complexioned "Aryan stock" from whom, in Howard's view, the Celts, Gaels, and Britons of the British Isles descended. Howard was influenced by the writings of Jack London, who referred to prehistoric Aryans in *The Star Rover* (1915) and "The Human Drift" (1917).

Aryara's Bronze Age culture suggests that he may have lived as long ago as the fourteenth century B.C.E. Aryara's appearance denotes what Howard called, in a letter to Lovecraft, the "light eyes and yellow hair...[of] the true Aryan complexion." His very name suggests that Howard envisioned him as the exemplar or prototype of "Aryanism." Howard once said that he had dreams in which he was, like Aryara, "a light-eyed, yellow-haired barbarian, resembling my real self but little."

Today, the concept of an "Aryan" culture and "Aryan" superiority is justly discredited as a scientifically invalid theory advanced to justify late-nineteenth and early twentieth-century xenophobia and racial intolerance. However, it was widely accepted in Howard's day. From a mutual admiration for Arthur Machen's horror fiction about "the Little People," Howard assented to Lovecraft's argument for a prehistoric occupation of Britain by a "Mongoloid" people who degenerated as they were driven into hiding by a successive wave of Celtic invaders.

In "The Children of the Night," Howard dramatizes this concept in the conflict between Aryara's folk, the Sword People, "tall and powerful, with yellow hair and light eyes," and the "early Mongoloids," the Children of the Night, who live in "squalid" burrows and have "deformed dwarfish bodies, yellow skin and hideous faces." Every detail in "The Children of the Night" is designed to emphasize the physical and cultural repulsiveness of the hero's enemies. They live in primitive huts "connected by underground corridors...like...a system of snake holes." In appearance they are "short and stocky, with broad heads too large for their scrawny bodies. Their hair was snaky and stringy, their faces broad and square, with flat noses, hideously slanted eyes, a thin gash for a mouth, and pointed ears."

This falls uncomfortably on the ear today, implying what we now would regard as thinly veiled racial invective in the allusions to "yellow skin" and "slanted eyes." However, it probably wouldn't have much fazed the average pulp-magazine reader in 1931. Attitudes now condemned as racist continued to influence American foreign and domestic policies at least into the 1920s, and persisted well into the twentieth century in pulp fiction.

Nor would the terminology have bothered enthusiasts of horror fiction who had read Arthur Machen. Howard's reference to "the hissing, reptilian speech" of the troglodytes mirrors Machen's reference in "The Shining Pyramid" (1895) to the "tones of horrible sibilance, like the hissing of snakes," articulated by the Little People on whom the Children of the Night are modeled. Machen's creatures, like Howard's, are a "ghastly yellow."

In Machen's story, two modern-day characters, Dyson and Vaughan, witness a secret ceremony in a natural depression by "things made in the form of men but stunted like children hideously deformed," in which a captive young woman is sacrificed. The sexual implications of Machen's story are squirm-inducing for modern sensibilities. The two men listen as "the voice of a woman cried out loud in a shrill scream of utter anguish and terror." The watchers' visibility is limited, but a description of "almond eyes burning with evil and unspeakable lusts" and a "mass of naked flesh" suggests rape.

The men make no attempt at interrupting the implicitly horrible ritual. Dyson later says, "I don't regret our inability to rescue the wretched girl. You saw the appearance of those things that gathered thick and writhed in the Bowl; you may be sure that what lay bound in the midst of them was no longer fit for earth." In "The Children of the Night," instead of two intimidated characters who watch an outrage impotently from the sidelines, on a helpless woman victimized in ways that Machen could only hint at under the restrictions of Victorian propriety, we have a vengeful, ax-wielding barbarian who plunges into the midst of his abhorrent enemies.

For a few pages, as O'Donnel remembers his existence as an ancient warrior in a deerskin loin-cloth, Howard provides violent, blood-splattering action that resembles the "butcher-shop carnage" (in the phrase of author and critic Fritz Leiber) of Conan the Cimmerian's more extreme exercises:

> I know not how many I slew. I only know that they thronged about me in a writhing, slashing mass, like serpents about a wolf, and I smote until the ax-edge turned and bent and the ax became no more than a bludgeon; and I smashed skulls, split heads, splintered bones, scattered blood and brains...

The reincarnation aspect of the tale, as a modern man remembers a past life in distant times, reveals the influence of *The Star Rover*: "a book that I've read and re-read for years, and that generally goes to my head like wine," Howard told a friend in 1930. London's protagonist remembers incarnations "through the ages known to-day among the scientists as the Paleolithic, the Neolithic, and the Bronze. ... Oh, I do see myself to-day that one man who appeared in the elder world, blonde, ferocious, a killer and a lover..." Howard's imaginative debt to *The Star Rover* would re-emerge even more emphatically in his stories about James Allison, which he would begin to write early in 1932 with "Marchers of Valhalla."

The protagonist of *The Star Rover*, convicted of murder, relives his past existences as he awaits execution by hanging. He ascribes the murder to "red wrath—a disastrous catastrophic heritage" of impulsive anger wired into his DNA. Howard's O'Donnel is evidently headed for the same fate. His distant memories as Aryara restored by the blow to his head, he determines to kill Ketrick, "the monster bred of the snaky taint that slumbered so long unguessed in clean Saxon veins." O'Donnel reflects, "Then they may take me and break my neck at the end of a rope if they will."

Howard's biographers in *Dark Valley Destiny: The Life of Robert E. Howard* (1983) dismiss "The Children of the Night" as "perhaps the least well-conceived of all the stories Howard sold in his lifetime." Readers more sympathetic to Howard's art would argue that, on the contrary, the disparate elements inspired by Machen, London, and Lovecraft are interwoven masterfully in this weird fantasy.

The story has been reprinted many times. If its racial aspects seem too daunting to overlook, you may approach it from another perspective. "They [O'Donnel's friends] say the blow I received affected my mind." Could they be right, and O'Donnel's obsession only a paranoid delusion?

Available in *The Horror Stories of Robert E. Howard*

People of the Dark

First published in *Strange Tales of Mystery and Terror*, June 1932

MAIN CHARACTERS

- John O'Brien / Conan
- Eleanor Bland / Tamera
- Richard Brent / Vertorix
- The Children of the Night

THE PLOT

John O'Brien, an Irish-American in England, loves Eleanor Bland, but she's torn between him and the Englishman Richard Brent. "I was going to simplify matters for her...and for myself," O'Brien decides. He follows Brent to a remote cavern, Dagon's Cave, carrying a revolver and intending to kill his rival. Legend holds that the cave was one of the last refuges where the Little People hid from the ancient Celts. Inside, O'Brien falls down a flight of tiny steps carved into the cavern floor. Knocked out, he regains consciousness in his former incarnation as Conan of the Reavers, a Gaelic pirate of some three thousand years ago.

Conan too has come into Dagon's Cave on a violent errand, pursuing Tamera, a girl whose British village his crew is raiding. Also in the cavern is Tamera's sweetheart and protector, the warrior Vertorix. The two Britons have been captured by the Little People, the Children of the Night, for sacrifice on the altar of the Black Stone. Conan sets them free, and the three flee through the labyrinthian corridors of the cavern. Separated from the other two after a skirmish with the Children, Conan emerges on a cliff to see Tamera and Vertorix trapped on an opposite ledge by their abhorrent pursuers. Their situation hopeless, the two Britons leap off the ledge to plunge to their deaths in a river far below as Conan watches remorsefully.

O'Brien comes to his senses again in the present day. He supposes that the Children of the Night have long ago passed into oblivion, but the Black Stone still rests in the cavern, and he thinks that he sees "a crawling something" scurry away from his flashlight. Following Conan's former route, he comes out on the remembered cliff, unseen by Eleanor and Brent on the opposite ledge from which Tamera and Vertorix had jumped millennia before. From their conversation, O'Brien learns that the modern man and woman also remember, now, something of their tragic lives from ancient times. Eleanor says that she realizes it's Brent she loves. "My soul was at peace," O'Brien discovers. And then the two lovers are attacked by the last remnant of the Children of the Night, a creature that has retrogressed to something "more like a giant serpent than anything else." A shot from O'Brien's gun sends the monster hurtling to its demise, saving Eleanor and Richard.

COMMENT

"People of the Dark" recycles motifs from "The Children of the Night." The most obvious are the shared background of

the Little People mythology and the first-person protagonist who remembers a past life in ancient times after a blow
to the head. Allusions to the Cthulhu Mythos appear both
places, although more peripherally in the two stories than in
Howard's core Mythos works.

But it would be a mistake to think of "People of the Dark"
simply as a case of Howard repeating himself. The earlier
background elements are not only re-used, but rethought and
re-purposed. "People of the Dark" can be read independently
of "The Children of the Night," but studied in sequence of
writing and publication, the two stories demonstrate Howard's
talent for elaborating on his favorite themes and creating rich
tapestries on which to weave heroic deeds.

With a swaggering, even ruthless hero named Conan, a
romantic interest, and plentiful action, "People of the Dark"
also marks an important step toward the emergence of the
author's most famous character.

The time of Conan of the Reavers would seem to be about
the ninth century B.C.E., when historians estimate that the
Iron Age began to dawn in western Europe. The Britons are
still forging their weapons from bronze, as suggested by
Vertorix's ax, which was also Aryara's favored weapon in the
earlier story. The Gaelic Conan carries an iron sword, perhaps
seized in a raid on the continent.

Vertorix swears by the god Il-marinen as did Aryara in the
previous story. Conan swears by the god Crom. Howard's use
of the names reinforces the idea that his characters live in
ancient and now-forgotten eras pre-dating the cultures and
more familiar mythologies of Greece and Rome. Il-marinen
appears in the pagan mythology of Finland's national epic, the
Kalevala, as a mythic god of the blacksmith's forge, but Howard
probably derived the name not from the Finnish source but
from Jack London's *The Star Rover*. In London's novel, the
protagonist's prehistoric self of the now-forgotten Aesir and
Vanir tribes worshipped Il-marinen as "our master-smith, our
forger and hammerer."

Crom, in turn, a deity of pagan Ireland, was derived from
Howard's readings in Irish history. Just as Conan with his
"massive naked limbs and powerful torso" differs in build from

the "rangy" Vertorix, the Britons and the Gaels worship different deities. The Britons and the Gaels are hereditary enemies who co-mingle peacefully only "in times of rare truce," but as they join forces against the loathsome Children of the Night, Conan and Vertorix find common ground in their respect for each other's bravery: "We worship different gods, reaver, but all gods love brave men," Vertorix tells Conan. This was a frequent theme of Howard's.

The passage of hundreds and perhaps even a thousand or more years between Aryara's time and Conan's is reflected in changes in the Children of the Night. Generally, they retain the same appearance. Of one specimen, Conan says, "Erect, it could not have been five feet in height. Its body was scrawny and deformed, its head disproportionately large. Lank snaky hair fell over a square inhuman face with flabby writhing lips that bared yellow fangs, flat spreading nostrils and great yellow slant eyes."

But the Children have reverted to a wholly subterranean existence in Dagon's Cave since Aryara's time, where their villages remained at least partly above ground. The typical specimen in Dagon's Cave is "able to see in the dark as well as a cat," and even though they remain "at least partly human," the creatures' sallow skin has become "scaly...and mottled, like the hide of a serpent."

This regression continues as "People of the Dark" returns to the present day and the final surviving specimen of the Little People comes "writhing its horrid shape up out of the darkness of the Earth":

> This thing was more like a giant serpent than anything else, but it had aborted legs and snaky arms with hooked talons. It crawled on its belly, writhing back mottled lips to bare needlelike fangs, which I felt must drip with venom. It hissed as it reared up its ghastly head on a horribly long neck, while its yellow slanted eyes glittered with all the horror that is spawned in the black lairs under the earth.

The Children retained at least a vestige of human appearance in "The Children of the Night." In this respect, the tale followed in the tradition of Lovecraft's "The Lurking Fear" (*Weird Tales*, June 1928), in which a reclusive family degenerates over time into "dwarfed, deformed hairy devils or apes." The Little People retained what we would now call their human DNA. With "People of the Dark," an added fantasy element appears when Howard suggests that the Little People have begun to develop reptilian attributes, first exhibiting scaly, mottled skin in Conan's time, and then regressing to crawling, venomous form in their final surviving descendant.

Howard also introduces another element not present in "The Children of the Night." This is the Black Stone, "[t]he ancient, ancient Stone before which, the Britons said, the Children of the Night bowed in gruesome worship, and whose origin was lost in the black mists of a hideously distant past." A "cryptic black object, carven with mysterious hieroglyphics," the object partly recalls the Black Stone of Howard's Mythos story, but it also suggests another inspiration from Arthur Machen, the title artifact from his story "The Novel of the Black Seal."

"Once, legend said, [the Black Stone] had stood in that grim circle of monoliths called Stonehenge, before its votaries had been driven like chaff before the bows of the Picts," Conan muses. In a 1930 letter to Lovecraft, discussing the history of the famed stone circle on England's Salisbury Plain, Howard already seemed to be nurturing that idea: "...doubtless the Celts did erect it, as you say, but we need not confine ourselves to actuality in our dealings with it."

With the name Dagon's Cave, the Texas writer appears to channel Lovecraft's fearsome Mythos entity. The path to the cavern is suitably gothic: "The approach to Dagon's Cave is always dark, for the mighty branches and thick leaves shut out the sun." However, in the absence of any supporting detail in the story, Howard seems to have chosen the name for its sinister connotation, and not as an indication that he intended to draw a connection to the Mythos.

The name "Conan" has caused confusion for some who read Howard's description of a grim but dynamic, sword-wielding freebooter, clad in loincloth and sandals, hair worn in a "square-cut black mane," who swears by Crom...and wonder why he's called a Gael and not a Cimmerian. When Howard wrote "People of the Dark" in October 1931, the creation of Conan of Cimmeria lay only four months in the future. It may be that by putting Conan the Reaver to paper, Howard was beginning to formulate the look and personality of his most famous character.

In a story already based on the idea of an eternal return of an individual from one incarnation to the next, or perhaps on the retrieval of deeply buried ancestral memories encoded into our genes, as critic Charles Collins once suggested, we can easily imagine Conan of Cimmeria, Conan the Gael, and John O'Brien as one personality in a progression of turbulent lives.

Available in The Horror Stories of Robert E. Howard

The Valley of the Lost

First published as "The Secret of Lost Valley" in *Startling Mystery Stories*, Spring 1967

MAIN CHARACTERS

- John Reynolds
- The Old People
- Saul Fletcher
- Jonas McCrill
- Bill Ord
- Peter Ord
- Jack Solomon

THE PLOT

The feud between the Reynolds and McCrill families in frontier Texas nears its bloody end as John Reynolds, the last surviving member of his family, eludes Jonas McCrill, four kinsmen, and their hired guns in the sun-blasted Lost Valley. Reynolds shoots one of McCrill's band, Saul Fletcher, from ambush. Thinking their enemy has fled after taking the shot, the others put Fletcher's body in the eerily named Ghost Cave and set off in pursuit. Reynolds goes into the cave to scavenge cartridges from Fletcher's corpse. Discovering a secret tunnel, he's attacked by the dead man, somehow reanimated. Reynolds breaks the revenant's back in a desperate fight, and as something whispers past him "like a ghostly wind," Fletcher falls, truly dead.

Reynolds soon learns that the cave is the refuge of the Old People, a dwarfish, deformed species whose ancestors had been driven into hiding thousands of years before to escape annihilation by invaders. The Old People had ventured into deeper abysses to learn "lost secrets, long-forgotten or never known by man." Losing their original physical attributes over time, they developed the power of telepathy to replace speech, and learned how to reanimate the dead. In a trance, Reynolds views a succession of scenes in which the Old People employed the dreadful talent to terrify, rout, and decimate the rare Indians and white pioneers who happened into the valley.

Seizing the creatures' crystalline idol of their serpentine god, the Terrible Nameless One, Reynolds holds his gun to it threateningly to gain safe retreat out of the cave. His human enemies return for Fletcher's body, Jonas McCrill riding off again for reinforcements to track Reynolds down. The others enter the cave. Screams and gunshots announce their fate in the clutches of the Old People. Reynolds uses dynamite from one of their saddles to close Ghost Cave, "[a]ll certainty and stability...swept away" now by the horrors he's endured. He commits suicide. Returning, Jonas McCrill finds Reynolds' body, the dead man's face "that of an old, old man, his hair white as hoar-frost."

COMMENT

In the early 1930s, Howard began more and more to concentrate his attention on the history and culture of his native Southwest. "The Valley of the Lost," which he submitted to *Strange Tales of Mystery and Terror*, reflects this shift in interest. He ingeniously re-imagines the notion of a degenerate, gnomish race and transplants it from the ancient forests of Britain to the rocky hills of west Texas, transmuting key elements of his earlier concept along the way.

Rather than prehistoric Celts, the early invaders who drove the ancestors of these troglodytes into hiding were the earliest wave of American Indians, the precursors of the Toltecs, apparently newly arrived over the Ice Age land bridge from Asia and "still close to the primal Mongolian rootstock." Where the Children of the Night were of human origin, even if a debased strain of humanity, the Old People descend from a species in general appearance "human—yet of a humanity definitely different from [Reynolds'] own." At best, the Children of the Night have rudimentary building skills, but the ancestors of the Old People lived in "a gigantic city of dully gleaming stone."

Drawn deeper into Ghost Cave by the sound of tom-toms, which "repelled him" but exert an "irresistible" lure (this is a familiar motif in Howard's weird fantasies, a hypnotic sound that lures the protagonist helplessly to a grisly death), Reynolds experiences a vision induced by the Old People. He gazes back in time to the primal metropolis, seeing it as "a city of lunacy to the normal human eye" in its weird architecture. Howard suggests that the shattered remnants of the early city still survive in Reynolds' day in standing stones of "a curious symmetry," like the monolith in "The Black Stone" and the Central American ruins in "The Thing on the Roof."

Already of strange appearance with their "curious peaked skull[s]," the original inhabitants of Lost Valley degenerate into a form similar to that of the Children of the Night, but even more outlandish in aspect than all but the final, almost fully devolved creature in the present-day segment of "People of the Dark":

> [Their] heads were peaked and malformed, curiously flattened at the sides. There was no sign of ears, as if their organs of hearing, like a serpent's, were beneath the skin. The noses were like a python's snout. ... The eyes were small, glittering, and reptilian. The squamous lips writhed back, showing pointed fangs...

Where the Children of the Night worshipped a relic called the Black Stone, the Old People venerate "the shining serpent, the Terrible Nameless One," represented by an idol "carven of some clear crystalline substance." Learning "lost secrets, long-forgotten or never known by man, sleeping in the blackness far below the hills," the Old People add this "black wizardry" to the "sorcery of their ancestors." They develop telepathy to replace speech, since "[d]arkness is conducive to silence," and learn how to reanimate human corpses. Like the wizard N'Longa in the Solomon Kane story "Red Shadows" (*Weird Tales*, August 1928), their sorcerers do so by transmitting their spirit into the dead body. Like the undead Zuvembie of "Pigeons from Hell" (*Weird Tales*, May 1938), these revivified bodies are sent forth on errands of murder.

Drawn as a quick-triggered feudist, gunman, and typically hard-fisted Howard protagonist at the outset of the story, John Reynolds is shattered by his encounter with the Old People. Once the adrenaline stops flowing after his escape from Ghost Cave, he's left as "a quivering shell of disrupted nerves," like a figure in a Lovecraft story. But the effects go beyond immediate, acute post-traumatic stress. "He had looked on ultimate foulness, and the knowledge was a taint which would never let him stand clean before men again..." The only way he can find relief is to put a bullet in his own head. "The Valley of the Lost" is one of several stories and poems in which Howard tragically foreshadows his own eventual suicide.

"The Valley of the Lost" was accepted by *Strange Tales of Mystery of Terror* but returned to Howard in October 1932 when the magazine ceased publication. It eventually saw publication in *Startling Mystery Stories*, Spring 1967. There it appeared as "The Secret of Lost Valley" as a result of confusion about the original title, but it has since been reprinted several times, correctly, as "The Valley of the Lost." Today it is regarded as one of Howard's pioneering efforts in the genre of the weird western.

Available in *The Horror Stories of Robert E. Howard*

The Little People

First published in *Coven 13*, January 1970

MAIN CHARACTERS

- Costigan
- Joan Costigan
- The Little People
- Ghostly Druid

THE PLOT

Two Americans, Costigan and his sister Joan, are vacationing on the English moors, in an area once and perhaps still haunted by the Little People of legend who were said to carry off children for sacrifice in olden times. Joan scoffs at the tradition and when challenged by her brother, who bets that she wouldn't spend the night at a nearby stone ruin despite her skepticism, she takes him up on the wager. Costigan regrets his impulsiveness and orders her to stay in her room. That night, he dreams that he's shaken urgently by a silent, white-bearded man. Awakening with a sensation of foreboding, he finds his sister's room empty, A night clerk tells him that Joan has gone out.

Costigan pursues and sees Joan ahead on the moor, surrounded by a horde of dwarfish, threatening figures. She seeks refuge at the nearby ruin, the remnant of a Druid altar, as the creatures bar Costigan's way when he rushes ahead to protect her. He realizes that he can't get to her in time to save her from harm, and utters a cry that echoes "down the long reaches of Time." The white-bearded man of his dream, a spectral druid, the ancient enemies of the Little People, routs the attackers and raises his hand to the Costigans as if in benediction, before he disappears.

COMMENT

Written before "The Children of the Night" but not published until long after Howard's death, "The Little People" articulates Howard's original conception of the Little People's origins before he had decided—after discussion with Lovecraft—to modify that initial assumption:

> "The 'Little People'' spoken of by Machen are supposed to be the descendants of the prehistoric people who inhabited Europe before the Celts came down out of the north.

> They are known variously as Turanians, Picts, Mediterraneans, and Garlic Eaters.

Otherwise, the Little People are imagined and described much as Howard would delineate the Children of the Night two years later, as degraded survivals of a "small, dark people" who fled underground before the invading Celts. The creatures who threaten Joan Costigan with a fate "of hideous evil... something foul and grim" are "short, dwarfish," with "gnarled limbs,...snake-like, beady eyes that glared unwinkingly,...grotesque, square faces with...unhuman features."

Howard clearly acknowledges his debt to Arthur Machen. Costigan is fond of "The Shining Pyramid" and discusses Machen's Little People mythology but without going into detail about the plot, lest Howard tip his hand too soon that his troglodytes will attempt to abduct Joan just as the "wretched girl" Annie Trevor was seized in Machen's story.

The casual racism of "The Shining Pyramid" with Machen's troglodytes showing "a Mongolian cast of features" is absent from "The Little People," perhaps because at this time Howard was still conflating the Little People with the Picts. It began to creep into "The Children of the Night" after Lovecraft sparked Howard's reappraisal of his initial theory. Costigan's brawl with the Little People has something of the violence repeated in the Bronze Age segment of "The Children of the Night": "features crumpled and bones shattered beneath my flailing fists..." But the mayhem in the latter story is amplified and described at greater length, as Howard there finds his stride in combining horror, fantasy, and action in the Conan style.

Costigan's seventeen-year-old "flapper sister" Joan lightly dismisses Machen and prefers Michael Arlen (1895–1956), a writer virtually forgotten today but popular in the late 1920s (even securing the cover on *Time* magazine in 1927) for *The Green Hat* (1924) and other novels about London's post-World War I high society. In a 1928 letter, Howard sneered at "these insipid sophists who happen to be sitting on the roof [of the] drawing-room of the world." The "Costigan" of the story is not to be confused with the other Costigans who were swirling around in Howard's imagination around the same time, including Sailor Steve Costigan of Howard's boxing stories, Steve Costigan who appears in "Skull-Face," Steve Costigan who represents Howard himself in the fictionalized autobiography *Post Oaks and Sand Roughs*, and Mike Costigan of "Spanish Gold of Devil Horse," who was named Steve Costigan in an earlier draft.

Available in *Bran Mak Morn: The Last King*

Notes

- Chronologically in terms of setting, "Worms of the Earth" (*Weird Tales*, November 1932) falls between the early Iron Age backdrop of "People of the Dark" and the present-day milieu of "The Little People." Enthusiasts generally assume that this Bran Mak Morn fantasy is set in the third century A.D., as Rome attempts to tighten its grip on Britain. Bran bargains with the Children of the Night to destroy a Roman outpost. As in "People of the Dark," the Children of the Night venerate the Black Stone. They are described similarly to their depiction in the other stories: "...broad strangely flattened head, pendulous writhing lips that bared curved pointed fangs, and a hideously misshapen, dwarfish body that seemed—*mottled*—all set off by those unwinking reptilian eyes." "Worms of the Earth" is traditionally ranked as one of Howard's most accomplished stories. It is surveyed by Robert Weinberg in his section on the Bran Mak Morn series in *The Annotated Guide to Robert E. Howard's Sword & Sorcery.*

Gaelic Fear

Howard's friend Harold Preece called him "the last Celt" for his deep interest in the history and accomplishments of the Celtic culture, and especially in the folkways and chronicles of Gaelic Ireland. Preece's fond memoir of the same name is published in *The Last Celt* (Donald M. Grant, 1976), Glenn Lord's wonderful bio-bibliographical volume about Howard. Filtering his mostly autodidactic knowledge of the subject through his imaginative affinity for ancient times and headstrong but often melancholy heroes, Howard turned out reams of stories revolving around black-haired, volatile Irish warriors of times past and distant lands present.

There are many examples among the towering characters who became fixtures in Howard's various series. Cormac Mac Art was a pirate in the sixth century A.D. era of King Arthur. Cormac na Connacht was a Gaelic chieftain of Bran Mak Morn's time through whose eyes the events of "Kings of the Night" are viewed. Black Turlogh O'Brien was an outcast Irishman in the Viking Age. Cormac FitzGeoffrey was an Irish-Norman adventurer in the Third Crusade. Black Terence Vulmea sailed the buccaneering Caribbean. Kirby O'Donnell sought adventure and treasure in Central Asia and Afghanistan at the turn of the last century. Sailor Steve Costigan and Dennis Dorgan boxed their way around the pre-World War II globe as pugilistic merchant seamen.

Other examples of Gaelic or modern Irish characters outside those series include Donn Othna of "The King's Service," perhaps a contemporary of Cormac Mac Art's; Conn the thrall, who fights alongside Black Turlogh in the novelette titled "Spears of Clontarf" in straight adventure form and "The Grey God Passes" as sword-and-sorcery; the Crusader and disenfranchised Irish king Red Cahal in "Sowers of the Thunder"; detectives Steve Harrison, Butch Gorman, and Butch Cronin; and prizefighters Mike Brennon, Slade Costigan, Bill Cronin, Kirby Karnes, Jack Maloney, and Jim O'Donnel. In his pseudo-essay "The Hyborian Age," Howard suggested that the Atlanteans of King Kull and the Cimmerians of Conan were the ancestors of the Irish Gaels. Within the Little People series, the Gaelic element was reflected in the shift of perspective from the blond, Celtic Aryara in "The Children of the Night" to the black-haired, Irish Conan in "People of the Dark."

Howard internalized the notion of Celtic identity in his writings and letters, suggesting that Irish DNA in his composition made him subject to impulsiveness, moodiness, and vindictiveness. In a March 1929 letter to Preece, he wrote, "damn the Milesian blood in my veins that makes me like driftwood fighting the waves and gives me no peace or rest..." As late as 1932, he sounded a similar note in a letter to Lovecraft. He apologized for what he viewed in retrospect as rudeness in an earlier missive, blaming his behavior on hereditary moods "coming down the line of my purely Irish branch—the black-haired, grey-eyed branch, of which, as far back as family history goes, both men and women have been subject to black fits of savage brooding."

In *Post Oaks and Sand Roughs*, written in 1928 but not published until 1989, Steve Costigan—not the Sailor Steve of the boxing stories but a fictionalized self-portrait of Howard as a frustrated, aspiring writer in small-town Texas—calls himself "a son of old America and old Ireland." At a football game, Steve tries to watch the plays with detachment but "[t]his he always found to be impossible, and blamed it on his fiery Celtic blood." Elsewhere Howard writes: "Steve Costigan was a black Celt, and there is no race which cherishes a hate longer."

Recent research by Howard scholar Rusty Burke casts doubt that Celtic or Irish bloodlines actually predominated in Howard's family history, but at some level, Howard seems to have believed that they did.

Howard's greatest enthusiasm for Celtic and Gaelic subjects spanned a period from 1928 to 1931, emerging on the front end from an earlier interest in primitive antiquity and shading on the other into his growing fascination with regional Southwestern history. Even as he left Turlogh O'Brien and Cormac FitzGeoffrey behind, his affinity for Irish heroes informed his western stories with their protagonists Bill McClanahan ("Vultures' Sanctuary") and Steve Corcoran ("The Vultures of Wahpeton"), in a tradition that places Howard's westerners alongside the iconic western heroes of James Warner Bellah, Louis L'Amour, Larry McMurtry, and Jack Schaefer with their Irish and Scots-Irish names. Harold Preece suggested a natural affinity between Celtic and Old West subjects in Howard's imagination, finding that "the frontier ruggedness of Texas certainly influenced his interpretation of Celtica."

While serving as an important component for his sword-and-sorcery and adventure stories, Gaelic settings and traditions also appear in several weird fantasies outside the established series.

If we can believe Howard, and in this instance why shouldn't we, a taste for horror inspired by Irish temperament and folklore was an early influence from the time of his boyhood. Howard confided to Lovecraft about African-American traditions he had heard as a child from his family's mixed-race cook. "But no negro ghost story ever gave me the horrors as did the tales told by my grandmother," he added.

"All the gloominess and dark mysticism of the Gaelic nature was hers," he said. He suggested that his grandmother had absorbed Irish traditions from her immigrant parents, along with African-American stories that she picked up by living in the Southwest: "My grandmother was but one generation removed from south Ireland and she knew by heart all the tales and superstitions of the folks, black or white, about her." Whether real or mostly self-imagined, Howard's professed Gaelic lineage placed him in company with other Irish masters of the supernatural, including J. Sheridan Le Fanu, Charles Maturin, Bram Stoker, Fitz James O'Brien, and Oscar Wilde.

The Cairn on the Headland

First published in *Strange Tales of Mystery and Terror*, January 1932

MAIN CHARACTERS

- James O'Brien / Red Cumal
- Ortali
- Meve MacDonnal
- Odin, the Grey Man
- A Dublin longshoreman

THE PLOT

James O'Brien, an American scholar, is coerced by his enemy, Ortali, into agreeing to help excavate a mysterious stone pile, Grimmin's Cairn, that stands on a headland on the outskirts of Dublin, Ireland. Ortali believes that the cairn contains riches waiting to be unearthed. O'Brien does his bidding because Ortali threatens to implicate O'Brien in the death of a colleague years before. O'Brien believes that the cairn dates from the battle of Clontarf in 1014, where the Christian Irish vanquished the pagan Norse—the veritable Ragnarok of Viking mythology, the death of Odin. He encounters an elderly Irishwoman, Meve MacDonnal, who gives him a holy relic, the ancient, lost crucifix of St. Brandon, to "shield you against the powers of evil."

A stone from the cairn, in O'Brien's pocket, serves as a conduit by which, that night, he dreams of a past life as an Irish warrior, Red Cumal, at Clontarf. During the "red flood of slaughter" on the headland outside the walls of Dublin, Cumal finds a one-eyed, grey-armored, fallen Norse warrior on the battlefield and realizes that he is the Viking god Odin, who took human form to lead the Norse in battle. Death-stricken from the stab of a spear inscribed with a cross, Odin mistakes the red-haired Cumal for a Norseman and asks him to put a sprig of holly on his breast to "free me from this fleshy prison." Instead, Cumal frantically buries him beneath a cairn on the headland that the Irish rename "the headland of the Grey Man."

O'Brien awakens, realizing that "the Grey Man's headland" is "Grimmin's headland," and discovers that Ortali has sneaked out to open the cairn. He follows, seeking Meve McDonnal and finding her headstone with the dates 1565–1640. Arriving at the cairn as a sprig of holly falls from Ortali's lapel onto Odin's uncovered form, O'Brien watches as the figure arises and swells into a "towering anthropomorphic form as dark as shadow and gleaming as ice." The monster strikes Ortali dead and approaches O'Brien, "shadowy, tentacle-like arms outspread." From the American's venerable crucifix, a shaft of light strikes the demon, shriveling it and sending it "fleeing back into the dark limbo which gave him birth."

COMMENT

"The Cairn on the Headland" approaches Lovecraft territory with its revelation of the mythic Odin as "a spirit of ice and frost and darkness." The being is only human-like in having assumed "the attributes of mankind." It actually is a tentacled entity from outer space that retreats before the light of O'Brien's cross "with a great rush of vulture-like wings."

The sign of the cross comes into play twice. The first time, a "spear with a cross carved in the blade" fells Odin in battle. "[N]o other weapon could wound me." The second time, St. Brendan's crucifix as a "symbol of the powers opposed forever against the fiends of darkness" puts the creature to flight, presumably forever.

The motif of the cross doesn't seem to have any intrinsic, emotional meaning for Howard as a representation of orthodox Christianity. More likely, he borrowed it as a convenient horror-fiction device, and in context it comports with his theme of a modern age represented by Christianity emerging from a dreadful "reign of blood and iron" under Viking domination. The sign of the cross serves a similar function as a weapon against malicious entities in Frank Belknap Long's Mythos story "The Space-Eaters" (*Weird Tales*, July 1928). There, a supposed excerpt from the English translation of the *Necronomicon* states that the cross "protects the pure of heart" from evil.

The idea of a blade imbued with occult killing power against a demon reappears in the first Conan story, "The Phoenix on the Sword" (*Weird Tales*, December 1932), written in March 1932. There, Conan slays a monster with a sword inscribed with "the emblem of the immortal phoenix." The idea may have stuck in Howard's mind from January 1932, when he sold "The Cairn on the Headland." Adding a supernatural element was one of Howard's fundamental changes in turning a previously unsold King Kull adventure into the inaugural Conan tale.

Red Cumal has blue eyes like Conan, but his red hair and beard set him apart from Howard's other Irish characters, who are usually black-haired and clean-shaven. His appearance serves a dramatic purpose, since the stricken Odin, "seeing mistily my red beard and the [stolen] Norse armor I wore, supposed me to be" a Viking. And so Odin discloses his true identity to the Irishman, enabling O'Brien to realize the danger of digging into the cairn.

The spectral Meve MacDonnel is one of Howard's strong maternal figures, like the benevolent witch Zelata in the Conan novel *The Hour of the Dragon* (*Weird Tales*, December 1935-April 1936). "She was tall and strongly made, with a strong stern face, deeply lined and weather-worn as the hills." Such characters may come as a surprise to cursory fantasy fans who have formed the incorrect idea that as a writer, Howard had little use or respect for the female gender, aside from concocting helpless princesses or slave girls to be rescued by Conan.

She also represents a recurring pattern of the wise elder who penetrates the mystic barrier between life and death to aid the hero, like the ghostly Epemitreus in "The Phoenix on the Sword" and the phantom Druid in "The Little People." Just as Howard's swordsmen are as likely as not to be swordwomen, his seers are likely as not to be seeresses.

The framing story strengthens the unity of the tale by reinforcing the theme of the Clontarf scenes. Bled by Ortali's ongoing blackmail, O'Brien suffers a "slavery bitter as my Celtic ancestors knew beneath the heels of the Vikings." The subplot of Meve MacDonnel aiding and protecting O'Brien across time or from beyond the grave provides an additional fantasy component to the tale.

Some critics surmise that "The Cairn on the Headland" was a rescue job from two earlier, unsold novelettes about the battle of Clontarf, or rather from one story cast first as a straight historical adventure ("Spears of Clontarf") and then rewritten to add a fantasy element. In the revised version, "The Grey God

Passes," also published in some editions as "The Twilight of the Grey Gods," Odin appears to two of the characters as a grim, one-eyed man. At the end, he is seen disappearing into the sky as "a vague, gigantic form...beard and wild locks flying," as the Irish win the battle over the Norsemen. "He flees the new gods and their children," intones Turlogh O'Brien.

The earlier story is gripping, but once the battle starts, it turns into a sprawling, Homeric epic related as a series of fights between individual warriors, like the *Iliad*. By dialing down the battle to five paragraphs in which the violence is related in passing as scenes in which "half-naked tribesmen...tore and slashed with helmeted warriors," by adding a framing story in modern times, and by incorporating a ghost and a monster, Howard produced a commercially successful scenario for his weird fantasy market. Both "Spears of Clontarf" and "The Grey God Passes" are available in paperback editions of Howard's works.

It is likely that Howard derived much of the background for the story from P.W. Joyce's *A Short History of Gaelic Ireland* (1924), which he owned. The Chronicles of the Four Masters, the Book of Leinster, and the Book of Lecan mentioned by James O'Brien are all referenced in Joyce.

Joyce called Clontarf "the last great struggle between Christianity and heathenism," echoed in O'Brien's description of Clontarf as "a war between the White Christ and Odin, between Christian and pagan. It was the last stand of the heathen." Howard was a master at selecting suggestive texts from his wide readings and from them, weaving his own wonderful fiction.

Available in *The Horror Stories of Robert E. Howard*

Dermod's Bane

First published in *Magazine of Horror*, Fall 1967

MAIN CHARACTERS

- Michael Kirowan
- Moira Kirowan
- Dermod O'Connor
- Kirowan's grandmother
- Sir Michael Kirowan (by reference)

THE PLOT

Kirowan, the narrator, is plunged into wrenching grief by the death of his twin sister Moira. His grandmother advises him to visit Galway, the homeland of his ancestors, to heal his sorrow.

There, he again hears the story of the murderous outlaw Dermod O'Connor, who terrorized the region in medieval times. Dermod was finally brought to ground by Kirowan's namesake ancestor, each dealing the other a fatal sword-blow. Kirowan's posse seized the dying outlaw and hung him from a tree on a cliff over the sea, as he swore vengeance on the Kirowans "for all time to come." From then on, the tree was known as Dermod's Bane.

A townsman says that Dermod's ghost is abroad on moonless nights: "...let you not walk in the cliffs over the sea by night," the townsman warns Kirowan, "for you are of the blood he hates."

One moonless night, as his anguish returns, Kirowan wanders up onto the hill where the hanging tree stands. A misty form appears and its "vague, sweet face" becomes visible. It's Moira's ghost. As it drifts away from him Kirowan blindly follows, and too late he finds that he has walked over the edge of the cliff, with death waiting on the rocks below. The ghost's face changes, becoming Dermod O'Connor's brutal, bearded visage. Back from the dead, he assumed Moira's appearance to lure Kirowan to a fatal fall. But then a "soft hand' clasps Kirowan's wrist, drawing him back to safety. Kirowan knows that the spirit of the real Moira intervened to rescue him. Now at peace, he is confident that he and she will meet again "in the world beyond."

COMMENT

Another Kirowan. The same Kirowan who appeared in "The Children of the Night," "Dig Me No Grave," and other weird fantasies by Howard? Some fans believe so, but it's unclear whether Howard meant a connection, or whether it was simply another Irish name, like Costigan, that he was fond of. The present author has chosen to regard them as different characters, but the reader is free to make his or her own assumptions. The evidence to support an association between one Kirowan and another is stronger in some of the stories than in others.

Treachery and internecine warfare resound through Howard's backstory about Dermod O'Connor, whose rampage occurred in a turbulent period toward the end of the twelfth century after "Dermot MacMurraugh [called "MacMurrogh" in some sources], driven out of Ireland by the O'Connors...brought in Strongbow and his Norman adventurers." "The history of the Irish race is one of betrayals," Howard once judged.

Dermod resembles a more brutal version of Howard's sword-and-sorcery hero Black Turlogh O'Brien, with all of Turlogh's qualities of misanthropy and none of his rough chivalry. "His [O'Connor's] hand was against all men, even his own house." Of Turlogh, Howard said in "The Dark Man": "All men's hands were against him." It's unfortunate that Howard lacked the luxury of writing an expansive story of Dermod's depredations.

In counterpoint to Dermod's retribution, the main storyline celebrates "a dead woman's love [that] conquered a dead man's hate." Howard ladles on the purple prose describing Kirowan's grief over the death of his sister, but probably not excessively so for the pulp readers of his time. Even today's hard-nosed readers may feel a little misty when Kirowan says that his sister's ghostly touch "loosened the frozen channels of my heart and brought me peace."

Howard's paean to the "gray old City" of Galway appears equally heartfelt, and perhaps even more poetically couched. There, "if you are of Galway blood, no matter how far away, your grief will pass slowly from you like a dream, leaving only a sad sweet memory, like the scent of a dying rose."

The late Glenn Lord found that Howard submitted "Dermod's Bane" to *Ghost Stories* magazine sometime during the period 1929–1931. The submittal may have been earlier in that span rather than later, perhaps just after Howard had succeeded in placing another tale with the magazine. "The Spirit of Tom Molyneaux" was published in the April 1929 issue as "The Apparition in the Prize Ring" under the byline "John Taverel." "Taverel" or "Taveral' was another favorite Howard name that appears in his stories almost as often as "Costigan" and "Kirowan."

"Dermod's Bane" failed to sell, perhaps because the Galway backdrop and the background material on Dermod's reign of terror were too extravagant for the magazine's formula. Like today's "reality" shows about ghost hunters, *Ghost Stories* pretended that narratives about phantoms were true accounts in recognizable everyday settings.

It may not have been a total loss. The death of a young Irish woman named Moira brings to a tragic conclusion the Turlogh O'Brien tale "The Dark Man" (*Weird Tales*, December 1931). Howard may have salvaged this emotional concept from the unsold story, channeling Kirowan's affection for his sister Moira, "pulse of my heart," into Turlogh's affection for his cousin Moira, "blood of my heart." If the element of a woman returning in ghostly form from the dead to save a loved one from violent death sounds familiar, chances are you're thinking of Bêlit's spectral appearance in "Queen of the Black Coast" (*Weird Tales*, May 1934) to rescue Conan from the attack of a monster.

"Dermod's Bane" finally saw print decades later in *Magazine of Horror*, during the time when the Conan and King Kull stories were beginning to trickle out to the spinner racks from Lancer Books. Even minor stories like this one were welcomed by fans, at a time when you could find Howard's published fiction only sporadically at the corner newsstand or drug store.

Available in *The Horror Stories of Robert E. Howard*

The Ghost in the Doorway

First published in *The Howard Collector* No. 11, Spring 1969, under the byline "Patrick Mac Conaire"

MAIN CHARACTERS

- Captain Turlogh Kirowan
- Conmac O'Sullivan
- Captain Balston
- Lady Nuala O'Brien

THE PLOT

Captain Turlogh Kirowan, an Irish rebel of the 1600s, spends the night in a ruined castle in County Clare while fleeing from Oliver Cromwell's Protestant English troops. He awakens to see

a man in medieval kilt and harness in the doorway, bleeding
from a mortal wound. The stranger warns that "the red-beard is
coming" before he falls noiselessly. Turlogh rushes over to find
that the intruder has vanished. Heeding the warning, he heads
for cover outside the castle just before a company of English soldiers rides up. In command is the red-bearded Captain Balston.
Kirowan sneaks away and later escapes to the Continent.

In France, Turlogh meets Lady Nuala O'Brien, whose family
owned the old castle. She tells him that he saw the ghost of
Conmac O'Sullivan, a Gaelic chieftain of the twelfth century.
Mortally wounded in a fight with Vikings led by a Norseman
called Red-Beard, he reached the castle to warn his kinsmen
that the raiders were coming. Repeated five centuries later, the
warning saved Kirowan's life.

COMMENT

"The Ghost in the Doorway" is imagined as "a memoir, in
Gaelic, of Captain Turlogh Kirowan, who held his commission
in the armies of France during the reign of Louis XIV, in 165–."
This would make him a younger contemporary of Alexandre
Dumas' Musketeers. He is one of Howard's many turbulent,
restless rebels of Irish extraction. The story proper, narrated
in first person and very short, follows three opening paragraph
that summarize Kirowan's career. Like the story of Dermod
O'Connor, it suggests the outline of an epic story that Howard
lacked the time and financial leisure to write.

Kirowan is no run-of-the-mill troublemaker but a leader
and strategist "foremost in all the plots and revolts against
English rule." He is sufficiently notorious that he "was well
known to [England's Lord Protector Oliver] Cromwell, both
for his valor and his craft." Howard's heroes of history had a
talent for making themselves known to the famous people of
their time, either negatively as in this instance, or in a positive
way like Cormac FitzGeoffrey with King Richard and Saladin,
or Solomon Kane with Francis Drake and Richard Grenville,
or in a more complex relationship such as Donald MacDeesa's
with Tamerlane in "Lord of Samarcand."

In his short essay "A Touch of Trivia," possibly written
around the same time as "The Ghost in the Doorway," Howard

rejoiced that "most of the oppressors of Ireland have come to an untimely end." The story calls Cromwell "a red-handed hypocrite," and the essay references Cromwell "with his bloody hypocrites." Howard tended to savor particular phrases that were likely to show up in his fiction, letters, and essays alike.

The oppression of the Irish by the English in relatively recent historical times (relatively recent, that is, by the yardstick of Howard's millennia-spanning fantasy fiction) is mentioned in the pirate story "Black Vulmea's Vengeance": "There were whole-sale evictions [of Irish tenant farmers by English landowners], with the military to see the job was done, and the Irish were mad enough to make a fight of it," the buccaneer Vulmea recalls of a skirmish in his Galway village when he was "a lad of ten." If the events of "Black Vulmea's Vengeance" occur at the height of activity by the buccaneers, in the 1660s or the early 1670s, Kirowan may be a slightly older contemporary of Vulmea's.

Kirowan's story, "taken from his unpublished memoirs, being a free translation, and leaving out the quaint chronology of the time," is related in fairly brisk prose. It has little of the purple adornment that marked "Dermod's Bane," with which Howard attempted to convey the narrator's emotional anguish over his sister's death.

Like the other tale, it is presented as a true story in the venerable tradition of "The Apparition of Mrs. Veal" (1706), attributed to Daniel Defoe; "An Authentic Narrative of a Haunted House" (1862) by J. Sheridan LeFanu; and "Some Haunted Houses" (1910) by Ambrose Bierce. As M.R. James once noted, these literary works followed an even older tradition in which "[v]ery nearly all the ghost stories of old times claim[ed] to be true narratives of remarkable occurrences." Howard's prose simulates the matter-of-fact style the reader would expect from a translation (presumably by a historian) of a memoir written by a military man.

One wonders whether, like "Dermod's Bane," the tale was also intended by Howard for *Ghost Stories*, with the "Patrick Mac Conaire" byline disguising Howard's name just as "John Taverel" did for the one story that he succeeded in placing with the magazine. Presumably, this was a strategy to advance the illusion that "The Ghost in the Doorway" was a true story by someone whose name would not be recognized from the contents pages of other magazines.

Glenn Lord's research found that "Patrick Mac Conaire" was used as a pseudonym only once, for this story, although Howard signed some of his poems as "Patrick Mac Conaire Howard" and "Patrick Howard." "Kirowan" re-appears as the protagonist's name, reinforcing the supposition that "The Ghost in the Doorway" was written in the same period as "Dermod's Bane" as another intended submission for *Ghost Stories*, in which Howard indulged his fascination with Irish history.

Available in *Pictures in the Fire*

Ghosts

Phantoms, apparitions, and visions appear in all three of Robert E. Howard's Gaelic-themed weird fantasies, as discussed in the survey above, and in four other stories with themes and settings unrelated to Howard's interest in Gaelic or Irish history and culture. Those four stories, discussed in this section, are "The Spirit of Tom Molyneaux," originally published as "The Apparition in the Prize Ring"; "Delenda Est"; "Restless Waters"; and "The Shadow of the Beast."

Also included here is "The Touch of Death" as a related tale about a return from the dead. Another included in this section, "The Shadow of Doom," involves precognition, a phenomenon often associated with ghost stories in "strange but true" accounts of supernatural marvels. An unfinished work, titled "Spectres in the Dark," ends before it becomes clear whether or not the phenomena described in the unfolding narrative actually are caused by ghosts in the traditional sense of the term.

The ghosts in two of the traditional spectral stories are beneficent, the third harmful, the fourth vengeful. In two of the stories, the phantoms help or support the protagonists. In the story of precognition, an apparition warns of a catastrophe yet to occur. All of the stories have points of interest for Howard fans, even if other readers are likely to find them inferior to the best ghost stories of other writers more closely associated with the genre, such as J. Sheridan Le Fanu, Ambrose Bierce, M.R. James, F. Marion Crawford, and E.F. Benson.

Ghostly visitations also occur in some of Howard's sword-and-sorcery stories. As noted above, Conan's great love returns from the dead in "The Queen of the Black Coast" to save the Cimmerian from a grisly death. In "The Shadow Kingdom," both King Kull and Brule the Spear-slayer are disconcerted by the restless shade of King Eallal, "who reigned...a thousand years ago." Kull feels "an icy hand at his soul" and Brule stares "in a blaze of pure horror" as the spirit walks past them silently with "an icy breath like a breeze from the arctic snow."

The encounter imparts what M.R. James would describe as "a pleasing terror in the reader," partially because of Howard's genius in setting the eerie scene and partly because we witness the apparition through his heroes' eyes. If valorous warriors like Kull and Brule are frightened by the ghost, are we likely to be any less terrified? The spell lingers in the reader's mind even though it shortly becomes clear that Eallal's revenant is more to be pitied than feared, like Marley's ghost in *A Christmas Carol*.

Howard's most memorable phantom may be the ghost encountered by the adventurous Puritan Solomon Kane on the moor in "Skulls in the Stars": "the thing began to take on shape, vague and indistinct. Two hideous eyes flamed at [Solomon]— eyes which held all the stark horror which has been the heritage of man since the fearful dawn ages—eyes frightful and insane, with an insanity transcending earthly insanity. The form of the thing was misty and vague, a brain-shattering travesty on the human form, like, yet horribly unlike. The grass and bushes beyond showed clearly through it."

The malevolent nature of the creature, and Kane's inability to harm it even as its "crooked talons" tear his flesh, are vividly described. The effect is hardly diminished by Kane's discovery that the specter has an understandable reason for its hatred. Ghostly revenge also propels two other fine stories about the Puritan swordsman, including another usually ranked among the author's best, "Rattle of Bones." The Solomon Kane stories are discussed in Bob Weinberg's *The Annotated Guide to Robert E. Howard's Sword & Sorcery*, and so they are omitted from the scope of the current book.

The Spirit of Tom Molyneaux

First published in *Ghost Stories*, April 1929, as "The Apparition in the Prize Ring," under the byline "John Taverel"

MAIN CHARACTERS

- Ace Jessel
- John Taverel
- Mankiller Gomez
- Tom Molyneaux
- Referee

THE PLOT

African-American boxer Ace Jessel is matched against another black prizefighter, Mankiller Gomez, the world champion. Ace's manager Taverel hesitates to put Jessel in the ring with the other fighter, "a born killer," but the situation leaves no choice. All other contenders have gone down under Gomez's crushing punches, big prize money is offered, and there's a matter of pride—sports writers are "accusing Ace of coward-ice" for not challenging Gomez.

Ace doubts his ability to beat Gomez, and feels he'll "need help mighty bad." His idol is the pioneering black bare-knuck-led prizefighter Tom Molyneaux, who fought the English title champion Tom Cribb in the early 1800s. Taverel spies Ace standing before his treasured portrait of Molyneaux, confessing his uncertainty about the coming match, and the manager remembers the claim by occultists that "statues and portraits have power to draw departed spirits back from the void of eternity."

In the ring, Ace displays fast footwork and lands several good punches, but Gomez's "style of fighting was such that when he was determined to annihilate a foe, skill, speed and science could do no more than postpone the eventual outcome." Going into the ninth round, Jessel is bloody and nearly beaten, but refuses to concede the match even after going down with a shattered nose and broken ribs. In desperation, hoping to inspire him, Taverel at ringside shows Ace the portrait of Molyneaux.

Through a haze of pain, Ace sees the ghost of the pioneer pugilist materialize beside him in the ring: "...to Ace Jessel, falling on the astounded Mankiller like a blast from the Arctic, Tom Molyneaux's mighty arm was about his waist, Tom's eye guided his blows, Tom's bare fists fell with Ace's on the head and body of the champion." Gomez goes down for the count. Although Taverel didn't see an apparition, the referee afterwards corroborates Jessel's account of "a broad, squat, funny-looking negro standing there beside" him, who presently vanished. Taverel leaves it to the reader to decide. For his own part, he now credits the occultists' assertion that "a portrait is a door through which astral beings may pass back and forth between this world and the next—whatever the next world may be."

COMMENT

"The Spirit of Tom Molyneaux" is a slight but interesting experiment in combining two of Howard's favorite enthusiasms, boxing and the supernatural. Originally written in third person, it appeared as a supposedly true first-person account in *Ghost Stories* magazine, around the same time that Howard had begun to land straightforward prizefighting tales in *Argosy* and *Fight Stories*. His vivid style gives the match between Ace and Gomez all the sweaty, blood-spattering immediacy of a movie.

"Readers of this magazine will probably remember Ace Jessel..." the short story begins. The folksy touch invites readers to suspend disbelief and accept that, indeed, they had seen Ace Jessel's name somewhere on the sports page. It would be interesting to know how many readers of *Ghost Stories* accepted the story as a factual account, and how many others recognized it as fictional but went along for the ride anyway. Lest you wonder how gullible people could get in 1929, reflect on today's long-lived "documentary" shows on cable TV about poltergeists, exorcisms, and haunted houses.

Howard's paranormal elements are out of the "strange but true" playbook, well chosen and strategically planted. As he watches Ace in front of Tom Molyneaux's portrait, and remembers the "age-old superstition" about portraits serving as a conduit to "the realms of the dead," John Taverel dismisses the notion—and then notices that "the canvas seemed to ripple slightly."

When Taverel displays the painting ringside, the canvas shakes "suddenly and violently." He adds: "A cold wind passed like death across me and I heard the man next to me shiver involuntarily as he drew his coat close about him." Cold air is usually associated with the appearance or presence of a ghost in parapsychologists' lore. In classic fashion, Taverel leaves room for doubt, not having seen an apparition himself: "...who knows the strange depths of the human soul and to what apparently superhuman heights the body may be lifted by the mind?" But the referee provides final, corroborating testimony: "It was a real man—and he looked like the one in the picture. He was standing there a moment—and then he was gone!"

Many present-day readers are likely to be put off by the racial aspects of the story. Described as a "great good-natured negro," Ace is unfailingly polite and deferential to his white manager, Taverel. His dialogue is rendered in patois: "Mistah John...I'll do mah best, but I's mighty afeard I cain't do it. Dat man ain't human." Gomez, a Senegalese, is described in what many will view as even more offensive terminology: "black savage"..."abysmal"..."ape-like, primordial."

For all that Howard's imaginative genius transcended his time, the reader should remember that, nevertheless, he was a writer of his time. In the controversial Howard biography *Dark Valley Destiny* (1983), L. Sprague de Camp and his co-authors judged that "[a]s with his fellow pulpsters of the period, Howard's handling of [black] dialect is crude." In fact, to be absolutely fair to Howard, stereotyped black dialect wasn't limited to pulp fiction. The dialogue in two critically praised and commercially popular novels of African-American life by white writers in the same era, DuBose Heyward's *Porgy* (1925) and Carl Van Vechten's *Nigger Heaven* (1926), is as dialect-laden as Howard's. Howard probably anticipated that his editors would demand the same popularly accepted style in his story.

If anything, a pulp magazine story featuring a sympathetic black protagonist in 1929 was a startlingly progressive achievement, however dubiously it might be viewed by today's standards. Ace Jessel reappeared in a non-fantastic boxing story, "Double Cross," unpublished until long after Howard's death.

Available in *The Horror Stories of Robert E. Howard*

The Touch of Death

First published as "The Fearsome Touch of Death" in *Weird Tales*, February 1930

MAIN CHARACTERS

- Falred
- Dr. Stein
- Adam Farrel

THE PLOT

Old Adam Farrel, a miserly recluse, has died. Falred, a neighbor, promises Farrel's physician, Dr. Stein, that he will stay the night at the dead man's house to observe the old custom of sitting up with the deceased. Falred scoffs at the popular notion of fearing the dead. But as the night wears on, his task begins to get on his nerves. A gust of wind disturbs the sheet lying over the corpse's face, and the sightless eyes seem to stare at Faired. Afterward, it seems to Falred that the corpse has become a conscious being staring at him through the sheet pulled up again over its face. Falling asleep, Falred dreams that the dead man has risen from the couch and started toward him. He wakens in darkness, now fearing that the dead man is "a terror, a monster, a fiend" who is creeping up on him. When he touches "something slick, cold, and clammy," he screams and falls. His body is found the next morning beside a pair of rubber gloves that Dr. Stein absent-mindedly had left the previous evening, "slick, clammy, and cold, like the touch of death."

COMMENT

"The Fearsome Touch of Death," which followed the extraordinary "Skull-Face" in *Weird Tales* two months later, must have been a disappointment for *WT* readers. The tale is very minor, apparently patterned after a similar story of psychological horror by Ambrose Bierce, "A Watcher by the Dead," but lacking Bierce's chilling, sardonic touch. Howard telegraphs the prosaic ending early on, when Falred is repulsed by Dr. Stein's "slick, cold, clammy" gloves before the physician leaves Farrel's house. Not even some flavorful Lovecraftian prose later on, as the increasingly overwrought Falred reflects on "man...[as] a wailing infant, lost in the night and beset by frightful things from the black abysses and the terrible unknown voids of space and time," quite redeems the story.

Available in *The Horror Stories of Robert E. Howard*

The Shadow of Doom

First published in *The Howard Collector* No. 8, Summer 1966, under the byline "John Taverel"

MAIN CHARACTERS

- Steve (narrator)
- John Harker
- Landlady
- Policeman

THE PLOT

Steve (the narrator) and his friend John Harker are walking late in a residential area of San Antonio. Glancing into a boardinghouse window, Harker is horrified to see a decapitated body inside. The two men summon a policeman and talk the landlady into opening the room. No corpse is found, nor any evidence of a murder. The landlady says the room has been vacant for two months. Months later, Harker moves into the same house and into the same room where he thought he had seen a corpse.

Passing by the house one year after Harker's fright, Steve glances in and sees a bloody figure in the room. It's Harker's headless body, as Steve is shocked to discover when he and the landlady investigate. An escaped inmate from a mental institution confesses to the murder. Somehow, Harker had experienced a vision or premonition of his own violent death.

COMMENT

Howard unsuccessfully submitted "The Shadow of Doom" to *Ghost Stories* magazine, under the same pseudonym of "John Taverel" that he had used for "The Spirit of Tom Molyneaux."

The short, slight story would seem to fit the magazine's style of fiction presented as fact, in a mundane setting. Perhaps the editors deemed the description of Harker's corpse, "drenched in blood—and the ghastly red stump of the neck," with his head lying nearby, "the dead lips writhed in a frightful grin of agony," too graphically gory for their readers.

The narrator, Steve, doesn't have a last name. If he did, it would likely have been "Costigan," Howard's obsessively favorite surname during that period. This Steve rooms in San Antonio rather than in "Redwood," the fictionalized version of Brownwood, Texas, where Howard's protagonist Steve Costigan rents a room in *Post Oaks and Sand Roughs* (1928), the author's semi-autobiographical novel.

The model for "The Shadow of Doom" seems to have been the homely weird stories of Ambrose Bierce, one of Howard's favorite writers. Bierce often set his stories in everyday, middle-class or rural settings and presented some as accounts of true hauntings and visions. "The Shadow of Doom" lacks Bierce's sure, unsettling touch, but it holds interest for Howard fans as an example of the author's use of a Texas residential backdrop, even though the San Antonio locale is immaterial to the plot.

Available in *Pictures in the Fire*.

Delenda Est

First published in *Worlds of Fantasy* No. 1, 1968

MAIN CHARACTERS

- Genseric
- Athaulf
- A Carthaginian
- Hunegais
- Thrasamund
- Vandal pirates

THE PLOT

The king of the Germanic Vandals, Genseric, sails from his stronghold in Africa on a diplomatic mission to Rome in 455 A.D. He and his captains are divided on the question of relations with the fading but still daunting Roman Empire. Hunegais argues that the Vandals "have but to stretch our hands and grasp the plunder of her." Thrasamund says that a great general of Carthage once thought the same—"I have forgotten his name"—but concedes that the man must have gone down in eventual defeat, since Rome endured.

Alone in his cabin, Genseric is visited by a purple-cloaked stranger who calls himself a Carthaginian. The stranger voices passionate hatred for Rome, warning the king that the devious empire has planted a spy in his entourage "who plots your ruin." Throwing down a coin as a gesture of good faith and picking up Genseric's girdle (belt), the stranger says that the traitor is the king's trusted scribe, Athaulf. He adds that he asks only one thing in return for warning Genseric: "Drench Rome in blood!"

Genseric finds Athaulf strangled with the girdle that the Carthaginian had picked up. The dead scribe had been writing a letter to the empress of Rome, revealing a plot to lure the Vandal fleet to destruction in an ambush. "Rome shall pay for this!" Genseric pledges. The stranger himself has disappeared, and a sentry says he saw no one leave Genseric's cabin. The Vandal king studies the coin that his visitor had given him. The Carthaginian's face is stamped on the coin, stirring Genseric's memories of having seen the same visage on ancient statues in Carthage: "Hannibal!"

COMMENT

The title of the story comes from a slogan popularized in Rome in the second century B.C.E. before the start of the Third Punic War in which Rome annihilated Carthage: *Carthago delenda est*—"Carthage must be destroyed." Howard places his story amid the historical turmoil on the Mediterranean in 455 A.D. in the declining years of the Roman Empire, and imagines a ghostly reason for the decision by the Vandal king Genseric to invade and plunder Rome that year.

A sword-and-sorcery fantasy without swordplay or sorcery (except as revealed in the supernatural nature of the purple-cloaked stranger), "Delenda Est" is anchored by Howard's deft portrait of Genseric as a shrewd, commanding barbarian king (like Conan) threatened by undercurrents of intrigue and treachery (like Kull). Where a needlessly verbose writer might have described the Vandal's boots-on-the-ground military leadership with paragraphs of exposition, Howard neatly does so in one telling sentence: "He walked with a limp; a Frankish spear had girded him in the leg long years before."

The mysterious Carthaginian speaks of his hatred of Rome, and undercuts the distinction often drawn between "barbaric" or unruly societies, and "civilized" or disciplined ones: "I have seen such a sack as not even you, barbarian, have dreamed of," he tells Genseric. "They call you barbaric. I have seen what civilized Rome can do!" Here we discern echoes of Bran Mak Morn's enmity for the Roman Empire in Howard's tales of the Pictish king, and of Howard's own professed emotions on the subject, which he said he was at a loss to explain: "...the old unreasoning instinct rises in me and I cannot think of Rome as anything but an enemy!"

Howard's interests in the ancient intermingling of different cultures on the borders of history are on display: "There was in [Genseric's] veins no trace of the Scythic blood which set his race somewhat aside from the other Teutons, from the long-ago when scattered steppes-riders, drifting westward before the conquering Sarmatians, had come among the people dwelling on the upper reaches of the Elbe." The historical and genealogical details are perhaps too plentiful for the short length of the story, but some background is necessary for setting the stage; few of us are well-versed in the later course of the Roman Empire. And fans will be carried along anyway by Howard's obvious enjoyment in weaving his tapestry.

The mysterious visitor from Carthage doesn't display any overt evidence of his spectral nature, aside from his comment to the Vandal that "forgotten ghosts burst their immemorial tombs to glide upon your decks," and his ambiguous remark, "I have come from a far land to save your empire." The former comment has a fine Shakespearean ring, recalling Horatio's lines in *Hamlet* that before Julius Caesar's death, "the graves stood tenantless and the sheeted dead did squeak and gibber in the Roman streets." The visitor's swift disappearance and his leaving behind material proof of his visitation (in the form of the coin that he hands Genseric, and the use to which the Vandal's borrowed belt is put) are traditional elements of the ghost story.

As a tightly written, subdued fantasy grounded in historical events, "Delenda Est" suggests the type of story that might have cracked John W. Campbell's *Unknown* magazine for Howard, had he lived to see its inception. By publishing novels of fantastic derring-do like Norvell W. Page's *Flame Winds* (1939), L. Ron Hubbard's *Slaves of Sleep* (1939), and Jack Williamson's *The Reign of Wizardry* (1940), Campbell seemed to be aware of Howard's lingering posthumous popularity, which he was prepared to serve by offering similar fare. It's sad that Campbell never had the opportunity to avail himself of the real deal. Howard's *Weird Tales* colleagues Robert Bloch, Henry Kuttner, Frank Belknap Long, and Catherine Moore all appeared in *Unknown*, and there's a fair chance that Howard would have, too.

Available in *The Horror Stories of Robert E. Howard*

Restless Waters
First published in *Witchcraft & Sorcery* No. 10, 1974

MAIN CHARACTERS
- Tavern serving boy (narrator)
- Captain Starkey
- Betty Starkey
- Jonas Hopkins
- Tom Siler
- Dick Hansen
- John Gower

THE PLOT
In the Silver Slipper tavern on a stormy coastal New England night in 1845, several regular patrons are gathered for dinner. Conversation reveals that short-tempered Captain Starkey is about to give his niece and ward Betty in marriage to an older merchant, Harmer. Betty doesn't want to wed Harmer, but Starkey is forcing her to marry because Harmer's money will save Starkey from bankruptcy. Betty still longs for her sweetheart Dick Hansen, missing and thought drowned. Whether Hansen is "[a]live or dead, I'm his till I die," she entreats. But Starkey, a brutal man who once hanged his first mate Tom Siler at sea for mutiny, angrily rebuffs the girl.

Too much strong drink shortens the tempers around the fire. Attorney Jonas Hopkins notes that Siler, before he was hanged, claimed that he was being executed not because of any mutinous plot, but because "he had learned what became of Dick Hansen." It transpires that Starkey had the young man shanghaied and reported dead to ensure that his plans to marry Betty to Harmer were not disrupted.

Worked into a rage, Starkey says that the matter remains incontrovertible because Siler is "in Hell with a noose around his neck" and Betty will be married before Hansen has any chance to return home. "No living man can balk me." As the wind howls at the window, the narrator, the taproom boy, feels a sudden chill "as if through a suddenly opened door, a wind from some other sphere had breathed upon me." Starkey stares at the window and suddenly falls dead. The narrator, the only other person present who glances at the window at that second, sees Tom Siler's spectral face with a noose around his neck.

COMMENT

"Restless Waters" has the atmosphere of a Robert Louis Stevenson ghost story, if Stevenson had ever grafted the mariners from *Treasure Island* onto one of his spectral tales like "The Body Snatcher" and "Thrawn Janet." Although the reader may infer that Starkey died from a heart attack or stroke brought on by his choleric temper and too much brandy, and not from shock at seeing Siler's ghost, the narrator seems convinced that a spectral visit truly occurred, as he remembers the events of the night years later.

The conversation-driven story builds its plot on a gradual accumulation of details relating to the hanging of Tom Siler and the disappearance of Dick Hansen. This format is similar to the structure of "Dig Me No Grave," with its clues patiently leading to the revelation about John Grimlan's dark pact, and that of "Delenda Est" as the identity of the visitor from Carthage is revealed. Although this format doesn't exercise Howard's basic strength as a writer of fast action, he plays fair in planting the details that gradually reveal Starkey's guilt and prepare the reader for the supernatural outcome.

His marvelous command of visual and physical description convincingly paints the atmosphere of the nineteenth-century waterside tavern, where locals congregate before a roaring fire while, outside, the storm-driven waves of the sea "beat frenziedly against the stark New England coast." But nature's violence soon finds a counterpart inside when first John Gower intervenes to prevent Starkey from striking the distraught Betty, and then as Starkey's sordid backstory emerges.

As in "The Spirit of Tom Molyneaux," an "unearthly coldness" accompanies the appearance of the ghost, and as in "Delenda Est," a thirst for retribution brings the phantom back from the dead.

The story was another of the several ghostly narratives that Howard wrote in 1929, presumably for submission to *Ghost Stories* after having scored a sale with "The Spirit of Tom Molyneaux." Like the others, it was unsold during his lifetime but—as if ironically, in a real-life triumph over the grave—it finally saw print decades later.

Available in *The Horror Stories of Robert E. Howard*

The Shadow of the Beast

First published in *The Shadow of the Beast*, 1977

MAIN CHARACTERS

- Steve (narrator)
- Joan
- Joe Cagle
- Harry

THE PLOT

Steve hurries from Texas to a southern lumber camp to join in the pursuit of Joe Cagle, a laborer who had attempted to molest Steve's sweetheart, Joan, wounding Joan's brother Harry when he intervened. Joan fears that the fugitive will return to make good his boast to rape her: "He will, too.... nothing but death can stop him." The chase leads Steve into the swampy backwoods, where he suspects that Cagle has taken refuge in the Deserted House, a ruined and reputedly haunted plantation manor. At least three men have died there in apparent plunges from an upper window.

Left afoot when his horse runs off, Steve goes into the old house amid "the whisper of bats' wings and the scampering of mice." He finds Cagle's corpse upstairs, dead from fright. A shadow falls across the moonlit wall, of "something inhuman." The shadow begins to move toward him, with nothing to cast it. Firing his pistol into it with no effect, Steve runs away as "huge, misshapen footprints" appear on the dusty floor. To escape, he leaps out the window.

When he regains consciousness, Joan is there, having come to find him when his horse returned to camp without him. She tells him that an ape from a traveling circus had taken refuge in the empty house twenty years before, escaping mistreatment. Found by his owners, he had fought recapture so fiercely that they were forced to kill him. Steve realizes that the shadowy entity was the specter of the ape. Fire destroys the old ruin, laying the savage ghost to rest.

COMMENT

The unique aspect of this story is the nature of the ghost—animal rather than human as in Howard's other tales of phantom visitations. Nevertheless, the protagonist's remarks about the supernatural are similar to those in Howard's other weird fantasies: "There are worlds and shadows of worlds beyond our ken, and bestial earth-bound spirits lurk in the dark shadows of our world..." The term "earth-bound" suggests the theory of parapsychologists that ghosts are doomed to remain in places where they died or in life suffered great emotional trauma—a familiar trope in popular cable TV series about ghost hunters.

The story also adds a little ghost lore to explain the only visible characteristic of the spirit: "Long has it been said that a ghost will fling a shadow in the moonlight, even though it be invisible itself to human sight." In Mary E. Wilkins Freeman's frequently reprinted story "The Shadows on the Wall" (1903), ghosts are manifested as unexplainable shadows, but any association with Howard's story is probably coincidental.

This being Robert E. Howard, well-known for his stories that pit Conan and El Borak against anthropoid foes, it comes as

GHOSTS

73

little surprise that the "bestial earth-bound spirit" here is the ghost of an ape. The frightening nature of the phantom is vividly depicted: a "broad, shambling figure, stooped, head thrust forward, long manlike arms dangling—curiously human, yet fearsomely unhuman." In the backstory of the mistreated ape, Howard mitigates the reader's horror at the ghost's misshapen appearance with pity for the cruelty it suffered in life, much like the revelation about the malevolent but pathetic revenant that Solomon Kane encounters in "Skulls in the Stars."

As an immaterial being, the phantom lacks the ability to inflict physical injury. All of its victims die of fright or from a panic-stricken plunge out of the house's upstairs window. Steve runs from the ghost more like a fear-stricken character out of Lovecraft than like a typical Howard protagonist. His fall to the ground is painful but, luckily, not fatal.

This lack of a physical confrontation between Steve and the entity gives the story an unresolved quality, accustomed as we are to fierce grapples between men and apes in Howard's tales. It also seems anticlimactic that Joe Cagle is already dead when Steve finds him. The early part of the tale prepares us for a fight between the two men, at least.

The story was written in 1929 and unsold in Howard's time. Perhaps he reworked elements of it into two other tales with similar settings and subplots. In "Moon of Zambebwei," first published as "The Grisly Horror," the protagonist comes to physical grips with an African gorilla god in the U.S. Deep South. In "Black Hound of Death," another southerner tracks an escaped murderer into the swamps and engages him in a bloody hand-to-hand fight. The murderer Tope Braxton in that story is black, as is the attempted rapist Joe Cagle in the present tale, although in some editions of "The Shadow of the Beast," references to Cagle's race have been excised.

Available in *The Horror Stories of Robert E. Howard*

Notes

- "Spectres in the Dark," an unfinished story, unfurls a series of strange but apparently unrelated incidents told to or experienced by the narrator, Steve. A young man accused of murdering his mentor claims that he only acted in self-defense when the other man attacked him, suddenly appearing as "a horrid Spectre from some other sphere." The authorities doubt his assertion because the victim was confined to a wheelchair and apparently incapable of standing. A broken-down prizefighter named Michael Costigan is haunted by "[s]hadows, like"; he thinks they are the ghost of an opponent whom he accidentally killed in the ring. Steve's sister Joan claims that her meek husband suddenly beat her with a riding whip. A stranger on the street strikes at Steve in panic, and then advises him to "[s]tay in the light and you'll be alright. They won't come out of the dark, not Them!" The fragment ends before Howard can explain whether the phenomena are associated with ghosts or perhaps linked to some other fantastic explanation such as demonic possession or sinister mind control. It is available in *Tales of Weird Menace*.

Science Fiction

Robert E. Howard's first published story, "Spear and Fang," could be considered a science-fiction adventure under the definition of fiction based on a premise that was scientifically plausible at the time of writing. The Stone Age setting reflected contemporary 1920s popular understanding of the early Cro-Magnons and Neanderthals, and it adheres to accepted scientific beliefs of the time more faithfully than, say, Edgar Rice Burroughs' "Sweetheart Primeval" (1915) and the movie "One Million B.C." (1940) in which cavemen and dinosaurs live at the same time.

It doesn't matter that discoveries in the intervening 90 years have invalidated much of the anthropological speculation on which the tale is based, any more than advancements in technology have ruled out Jules Verne's novels as pioneering SF.

"Spear and Fang" appeared in *Weird Tales* for July 1925, a year before the debut of *Amazing Stories*, the first pulp magazine fully devoted to science fiction. A few years later, as *Amazing Stories* was joined on the newsstands by *Wonder Stories* and *Astounding Stories*, "scientifiction" began to be recognized as a specific genre distinct from supernatural fantasy. By the early and mid-1930s, writers such as Robert Bloch, Edmond Hamilton, David H. Keller, Henry Kuttner, Murray Leinster, Frank Belknap Long, C.L. Moore, Clark Ashton Smith, Donald Wandrei, Manly Wade Wellman, and Jack Williamson were as likely to be found in the science-fiction magazines as in *Weird Tales* and *Strange Tales of Mystery and Terror*. Even H.P. Lovecraft, who generally disdained the science-fiction pulps, appeared in *Amazing* and *Astounding*.

Howard had a tentative brush with the field in 1933 when he sent "The Valley of the Lost" to *Astounding* after the story's originally intended market, *Strange Tales*, folded. The associate editor, Desmond Hall, sent a rejection, saying that *Astounding* was no longer accepting "any stories of the weird type," but he invited Howard to try something in the line of science fiction. Howard demurred, however, telling his friend August Derleth that "there is so little of the scientist about my nature that I feel no confidence in my ability to write scientific fiction convincingly." Besides, he contended, "the average pseudo-scientific tale...is pretty poor stuff." According to the dean of Howard studies, the late Glenn Lord, there is no evidence that Howard ever followed up with a submission.

Nevertheless, a few of Howard's tales can be classified as science-fiction, in which fantastic events take place on another planet, in the future, or in a terrestrial setting where advanced technology is employed. One such work was a chapter that Howard contributed to "The Challenge from Beyond," a collaborative story involving mind transfer between an alien and a human. It appeared in a semi-professional publication, *Fantasy Magazine*, in 1935.

A handful of other stories fit more or less comfortably under the category of science fiction. Some perhaps were written after Howard engaged Otis Adelbert Kline as his agent in 1933 with the hope of finding new markets for his work. Despite Howard's stated disinclination to write science fiction, he noted admiringly in a 1935 letter to Lovecraft that Street & Smith, whose family of pulps included *Astounding*, "pays good rates...and pays promptly." He had recently cracked Street & Smith's *Top-Notch* with four adventure stories featuring Francis X. Gordon and Kirby O'Donnell. However, none of Howard's other science fiction sold during his lifetime, and the most ambitious work along those lines, the novel *Almuric*, never advanced to completed form.

As science-fiction pulps increased in number and variety through the 1930s and into the next two decades, would Howard have made another run at the market they offered? It is tempting to speculate on that question. Many if not most leading Howard enthusiasts believe that his future lay in regional literature, had he lived longer, and that he might have left fantastic fiction behind altogether once he made his mark with an epic narrative about his native Southwest. Reading Howard's enthusiastic letters about the history and culture of Texas, it's entirely reasonable to speculate that he might eventually have written a big, sweeping novel to sit on the same shelf with Larry McMurtry's *Lonesome Dove* (1985) and Stephen Harrigan's *The Gates of the Alamo* (2000).

On the other hand, Howard had a deep attachment to imaginative fiction that persisted through his successes in two other genres, boxing stories and humorous westerns. The wave of technologically oriented, problem-solving science fiction ushered in by John W. Campbell Jr. in 1939, when he assumed editorship of *Astounding*, might not have ideally suited Howard's talents. Still, Campbell had a knack for attracting and nurturing other writers theretofore associated with *Weird Tales*, and one of his standard-bearers through the late 1930s and '40s was a pulpster who seemed as unlikely a Campbell man as Howard—L. Ron Hubbard.

The expansion of SF in the 1940s saw competition from pulps like *Planet Stories* and *Startling Stories* that were less technologically inclined than Campbell's *Astounding*, and more extravagant and swashbuckling in scope. Would the call have gone out for Howard to trade in Conan's sword for a raygun, and swap his Hyborian Age backdrop for sagas of restless adventurers on a Mars or Venus like the ones in Leigh Brackett's Eric John Stark novelettes? It seems the editors would have been receptive, given that thinly disguised variations on Conan appear in Brackett's "Queen of the Martian Catacombs" and "Lorelei of the Red Mist." A partnership with the science-action pulps could have meant a steady paycheck for the Texas author. But that's the world of might-have-been, not the real world that sadly was, in which Howard was long departed by the time those markets came into being.

Spear and Fang

First published in *Weird Tales*, July 1925

MAIN CHARACTERS

- A-aea
- Ga-nor
- Ka-nanu
- The Neanderthal

THE PLOT

The Cro-Magnon girl A-aea loves Ga-nor, a primitive but talented artist who adorns the tribal caves with his paintings. In turn, the councilor's son Ka-nanu lusts after the girl. He accompanies her as she goes for water, professing to safeguard her from a "gur-na," a man-ape or Neanderthal, whose footprint has been seen nearby. But once out of everyone else's sight, Ka-nanu's real intentions become clear as he seizes her.

At that moment the gur-na attacks, "a hairy, misshapen, frightful thing." It brutally kills Ka-nanu and grabs A-aea, carrying her off to his cave. There he torments her with "fiendish glee," but Ga-nor comes to the rescue. The two fight as the Neanderthal "set[s] himself to break his foe to pieces." The Cro-Magnon works free from the creature's hold and splits its head with his ax. He embraces the adoring A-aea, saying, "What I have fought for I will keep."

COMMENT

"Spear and Fang" was accepted by *Weird Tales* in late fall 1924 and published several months later. This was Howard's first professionally published fiction, slight but briskly and colorfully written. In the fictionalized autobiography *Post Oaks and Sand Roughs*, Howard's alter-ego Steve Costigan submits his story "Spear and Talon" to *Bizarre Stories* magazine, and its publication is "a pinnacle in Steve's life." We can assume that Howard had the same gleeful reaction in seeing his name for the first time on the contents page of a favorite magazine.

In the opening paragraph of "Spear and Fang," Howard assesses one of Ga-nor's cave paintings: "The result was crude, but gave evidence of real artistic genius, struggling for expression." The same might be said of the story itself. Even in this early effort, his mastery of describing a scene in brief, telling detail and depicting violent physical action is obvious.

Subtle but clever asides about the customs of Neolithic life abound, adding verisimilitude. When Howard says that "[n]o ocher tattooing tinted [A-aea's] cheek, for she was still unmated," he reminds readers that the story is set in a time and place far from their own, when tattooing was as rare in American society as it is common today. And then, with fine satirical timing, he suggests that in the basics, modern American culture of the Prohibition Era had hardly advanced from that of the Stone Age: "The more primitive a race, the more intolerant their customs. Vice and licentiousness may be the rule, but the appearance of vice is shunned and condemned."

Ka-nanu starts off as an unsympathetic character, but he redeems himself when the chips are down. As the Neanderthal attacks, "Ka-nanu, white-lipped and horrified, dropped A-aea to the ground and told her to run" while he interposes himself between. This gives the young woman a chance to escape as Ka-nanu engages in what he must know to be futile resistance to the vastly stronger monster. Even Howard's deepest-dyed villains sometimes rise to moments of heroism and nobility.

If not as protracted and viscerally compelling as Howard's later scenes of hand-to-hand fighting between Conan and fierce apes and ape-men, the battle between Ga-nor and the gur-na nevertheless foreshadows those memorable encounters in the Cimmerian's saga. The similarity in syllables between "Ga-nor" and "gur-na" prompts speculation: was Howard cynically implying that, in essence, there was little evolutionary difference between his Cro-Magnons and Neanderthals, after all? In their struggle to gain and maintain supremacy, the Cro-Magnons are hardly any more forbearing or forgiving than their intellectually inferior foes: "And ever the Cro-Magnon men trailed them [the Neanderthals] down and slaughtered them, until sullenly they had withdrawn far into the deep forests."

However, the similarity between "Ga-nor" and "gur-na" more likely resulted from Howard's tendency to use sound-alike names in the same story, as he often did, than from any conscious attempt at social commentary in this instance. As a natural poet, he may have liked how particular syllables rolled off the tongue.

The warfare between the Neanderthals and the conquering Cro-Magnons recalls Howard's later backdrop of enmity between the Little People and the conquering Celts. Like the retreat of the Little People underground, the Neanderthals have "withdrawn far into the deep forests." Pursuing warriors and wandering children occasionally enter the forests but never return, winding up as food for the other species. Like the Little People, the "savage, bestial, and cannibalistic" Neanderthal are remembered through later generations of humans as semi-legendary beings "in tales of ogres and goblins, of werewolves and beast-men."

"Spear and Fang" displays Howard's interest—formed early in his youth and lasting throughout his career—in the mysteries of the prehistoric past. His portrait of the Cro-Magnon race, "which came from no man knows where," contending against gorilla-like Neanderthals with "great, immensely long arms" and "short, gnarled legs," is outdated by modern science. However, it was consistent with popular speculation of his day.

As he worked toward the creation of King Kull over the next few years, Howard began to introduce more fantastic elements into his vision of humankind's origins. In a 1928 letter, he revisited the question of how the Cro-Magnons may have originated. "Suddenly their remains are supplanting the Neanderthal Man, to whom they have no ties of kinship whatever." Noting occultist beliefs in a lost continent of Atlantis, he suggested perhaps the Atlanteans were "the ancestor of the Cro-Magnon man, who by some chance, escaped" the primeval inundation. Although occultists like those in the school of Theosophy proposed a sophisticated level of culture for Atlantis, Howard flatly said, "I doubt that."

Howard seems to have adopted some of these concepts in fictional form from ideas proposed as fact by the Theosophists. Similar material appears in Howard's ruminations about the Picts in the Bran Mak Morn series. In addition, these conjectures took root in the Kull stories, in which Howard proposed a primitive level of civilization on Atlantis in his mythic Pre-Cataclysmic Age. The name "Ka-nanu" even reappeared in two Kull stories, minus the hyphen, as the name of a Valusian councilor.

Whereas in "Spear and Fang" Howard suggests that legends of "werewolves and beast-men" were simply distorted memories of the Neanderthals, the Kull stories populate the primeval world with uncanny creatures in fact: "...the bird-women, the harpies, the bat-men, the flying fiends, the wolf-people, the demons, the goblins," and the "snake-people [who] were the last to go" in retreat before human conquest. The "wolf-people" concept also surfaced in two tales about the haunted cavalier De Montour (discussed later in this guide), and "the flying fiends" perhaps in the Solomon Kane adventure "Wings in the Night" and the James Allison fantasy "The Garden of Fear."

Enthusiasts embrace the idea (credited to the late Steve Tompkins by Rusty Burke) that all of Howard's sword-and-sorcery expresses a common mythology of his invention that underlies all the tales of Conan, Kull, Bran Mak Morn, Cormac Mac Art, and more. "Spear and Fang" sits at least at the periphery of that vast saga. It's less overtly fantastic than the author's most celebrated work but interpretable (if you squint a little) as filling in a gap between the age of Kull and that of Bran Mak Morn.

Available in *Pictures in the Fire*.

Almuric

First published in *Weird Tales*, May, June/July, and August 1939

MAIN CHARACTERS

- Esau Cairn
- Altha
- Queen Yasmeena
- Thab the Swift
- Ghor the Bear
- Khossuth Skull-splitter
- Gutchluk Tigerwrath
- Logar of Thurga
- Gotrah the Major-domo

- Than Swordswinger
- Bragi of Khor
- Professor Hildebrand
- People of Koth
- People of Khor
- The Akkis

THE PLOT

Fleeing from the law after killing the ruthless political boss of an unnamed metropolis, Esau Cairn happens upon the laboratory of Professor Hildebrand. The scientist has developed the Great Secret, a device or process for teleportation. His only alternative being the certain ignominy of conviction and execution for murder, Cairn agrees to be transported to a "wild, primitive, and strange planet," Almuric. Materializing naked and weaponless, Cairn encounters a hairy, truculent brute against whom he comes to blows, finally overcoming the other's greater size through his knowledge of boxing. Some time later he saves another primitive tribesman from a saber-tooth, fleeing when the stranger's companions attack.

Captured by the people who live in the walled city of Koth, he finds that although a man of uncommon brawn and strength on earth, he's an anomaly among these even larger, hairy primitives of Almuric, called Guras. He begins to win friends nevertheless, and is inducted into the tribe after winning a grueling wrestling match against another tribesman, Ghor the Bear, who had never been vanquished before in a contest. He learns that the people of Koth are only one of several isolated, mutually hostile tribes of barbarians on the planet. As a species, all are known as "Guras." Far to the south live the Yagas, winged humanoids who periodically steal women from the human tribes. Beyond lies the Girdle, a towering rampart of rock that sunders the known world from an unknown southern hemisphere.

On a solitary hunting trip, Cairn saves the Kothic maiden Altha from a great, wingless, predatory bird. The girl has fled the tribe, unhappy with the constraints on women in her barbaric society. Esau decides she's better off back home than

SCIENCE FICTION   83

wandering in the dangerous wilderness, but before he can set off with her, they're attacked by Yagas and Altha is borne off. Pursuing, he discovers that the winged men have been killed by even more demonic adversaries, a race of ghouls. Altha has fled, and Esau, finding her, saves her from the ghouls. Before they can return to Koth, they are intercepted by the enemy tribe from the city of Thurga, ruled by Logar, who it turns out is the barbarian whom Cairn first met in his advent on Almuric. He bears a grudge from the fight. Yagas attack the city, and Logar attempts to kill Esau, but the Earthman slays him instead just before the raiders abduct Cairn and Altha. They bear their captives off to their "black citadel of Yugga, on the rock Yuthla, by the river of Yogh, in the land of Yagg."

The evilly beautiful queen Yasmeena becomes fascinated by Cairn, who escapes Yugga to summon help when he learns that she plans to sacrifice Altha as a Virgin of the Moon. Esau encounters a war party from Koth that has set out to battle an enemy expedition from Khor. When the Earthman entreats the two opposing forces to join in a march on Yugga, Bragi, the chief of Khor, objects, but is struck down by one of his own men, Than, the warrior whom Esau had saved from the saber-tooth months before. The combined barbarian army marches on Yugga, invading the citadel in a pitched battle. Yasmeena, seeing defeat, releases a colossal, electricity-spewing monster. Esau slays the creature on the battlements, and it and he plunge five hundred feet to the river below. Rid of the Yagas, the formerly rival tribes swear friendship. Cairn elects to remain with Altha and the folk of Koth as an adopted son of Almuric.

COMMENT

Almuric was published in *Weird Tales* three years after Howard's death, and a "coming next month" teaser in the magazine had this to say, in part:

> Robert E. Howard, at the time of his tragic death, was working on a new novel for *Weird Tales*. He had completed a rough first draft, and nearly completed a revision which was to be his final version. The bullet which crashed into his brain prevented the author from finishing this, his last story. ... Therefore we have pieced together the nearly completed final

draft that Howard wrote with the final pages of Howard's rough first draft, which contains a smashing denouement.

There seems to be consensus by Morgan Holmes, Mark Finn, and other enthusiasts that the *Weird Tales* blurb was misleading in suggesting that Howard was still working on the novel "at the time of his tragic death." In a May 1936 letter to August Derleth, Howard said that "I haven't written a weird story for nearly a year." Instead, he may have started *Almuric* after retaining Otis Adelbert Kline as his agent in 1933, as an effort to enter the "sword-and-planet" school of science fiction in which Kline had been successful. The templates for the genre were Edgar Rice Burroughs' novels of Mars, three of which were in Howard's library.

Howard may have learned or decided that trying to write a full-length novel in a new genre without an assured sale required more time and effort than it was worth, and put it away to concentrate on surer returns with Conan and the humorous westerns that he had begun to sell with regularity. On the basis of existing textual evidence in the absence of any surviving manuscripts, those who have studied the question speculate that at least the ending of the published story was contributed by someone else. After establishing that Esau Cairn was a misfit on Earth, too "primitive in his passions" to be constrained by the restrictions of "machine-made civilization," the novel ends with Cairn pledging to "instill some of the culture of my native planet" into the more congenial, barbaric society of Almuric. Some fans speculate that Kline wrote the final chapters, but Morgan Holmes and others suggest Otto Binder (1911–1974), a prolific science-fiction pulp writer (and later a prominent script-writer for comic books), who worked for Kline's agency at the time. But the question is open for debate. It's a pity that we know so little about *Almuric*, which even in its current state offers much to admire.

In Esau Cairn, known as "Ironhand" after his adoption by the people of Koth, Howard offers a character arguably even tougher than Conan. The strongest man on his native planet, where he unintentionally injured his opponents on the gridiron and in the ring because "he forgot to control his powers," Esau finds himself in a new, alien environment where he's matched against bigger, stronger foes. "Are you a man or a woman?" derisively asks the first Gura he meets. Ironically, in that first fight, he prevails not on the basis of brute strength alone but because he applies a strategic fighting technique: "The only thing that saved me was the fact that my antagonist knew nothing of boxing." Eventually, surviving out in the wild, he further builds up his strength and endurance to the point where he's able to meet the Guras on their own terms.

Clearly, Cairn is an idealized self-portrait of Howard as a native of the American Southwest "distinctly out of place" in his native society. Howard's letters indicated a similar alienation as an imaginative, creative artist in a mostly uncongenial rural, small-town environment. Esau is estranged from everyday life because his "physical body and mental bent leaned back to the primordial," like one of the unconquerable supermen created by Howard's idol Jack London. Esau's grueling contests against his opponents on Almuric are described in much the same sweaty, bloody terms that Howard used to describe his pick-up boxing matches in his letters and in his fictionalized autobiography *Post Oaks and Sand Roughs*. It may not be coincidental that, in the Book of Genesis, Esau—"a skillful hunter, a man of the field" like Ironhand on Almuric—had a father named Isaac, as Howard did.

In the voice of Cairn, Howard articulates sympathy for the women of Koth which, by extension, may represent the author's own reservations about gender inequality in the real world. Although "carefully guarded and shielded both from danger and from the hard work that is the natural portion of the women of Earthly barbarians," they have no authority in tribal affairs, they are mostly made subservient to the men, and their duties mainly are confined to "child-bearing and child-rearing." Altha is as much a misfit in her native society as Esau in his, for a reason that seems even closer than Cairn's to Howard's own introspective, sensitive personality: "I do not fit, somehow, as the others do. I bruise myself on [life's] rough edges. I look for something that is not and never was."

Howard draws on a familiar element of his fiction in contrasting a vulnerable young woman who represents stability and domesticity (Altha) with a dark-complexioned, decadent, sadistic, but seductively beautiful woman (Yasmeena). In this as in other characters and situations in *Almuric* that mirror elements he'd already employed in other stories (such as the cruel winged Yagas who recall the creatures in the Solomon Kane story "Wings of the Night"), Howard may have been trying to make the writing of a novel easier. I advanced the same theory years ago for the Conan novel *The Hour of the Dragon*, which recycled "greatest hits" from earlier Conan stories. The unrefined state of *Almuric* is reflected in an uneven pace, which slows in chapter four to load in several pages of exposition about the geography and societies of the primitive planet, circles back on itself in chapters six through eight when the Yagas capture Altha twice, and then speeds to a conclusion in the final chapter.

Lengthy exposition is often encountered in this type of old-fashioned sword-and-planet epic—Edgar Rice Burroughs' cornerstone novel in his Martian series, *A Princess of Mars*, is an example—and perhaps unavoidable. In *Almuric*, some of the exposition sets the stage for later scenes. Esau is told of "dog-headed monstrosities skulking beneath the ruins of nameless cities." Two chapters later, he saves Altha from an attack by the creatures. Other aspects of Almuric remain unexplored or teasingly vague, perhaps planted as clues to sequels that Howard would have written had he scored a sale with *Almuric* at the time.

Science-fiction writer Robert Silverberg once described the novel as "fun to read, easy to forget, a minor work in the Howard canon," sympathetically noting the bumps that it encountered on the way to posthumous publication. Fans may disagree about the rating of "minor" and may be inclined, instead, to find it worthy of substantial attention as Howard's colorful attempt to re-imagine his sword-and-sorcery as science fiction in the Burroughs and Kline tradition. And older fans may remember it fondly as an early Robert E. Howard paperback byline, when Donald A. Wollheim and Ace Books published it in 1964 to capitalize on the renewed popularity of Edgar Rice Burroughs and sword-and-planet genre in the early 1960s. Several reprints have followed, including the first hardcover edition, issued by Donald M. Grant in 1975, along with adaptations in comic-book form.

Available in Adventures in Science Fantasy

King of the Forgotten People

First published as "Valley of the Lost" in *Magazine of Horror*, Summer 1966

MAIN CHARACTERS

- Jim Brill
- Richard Barlow
- Lala Tzu
- People of Khor
- Tonkinese servants
- Togrukh Khan
- Mongolian bandits

THE PLOT

Traveling to the Gobi Desert to find Richard Barlow, a missing scientist and explorer, Jim Brill fends off attacks by Mongolian bandits and genetically engineered giant spiders before happening on the lost city of Khor. There, Barlow has set himself up as a tyrannical ruler, "Ak Khan," the White King, a priest of the god Erlik. Barlow has cowed the superstitious folk of Khor with his advanced scientific devices, which they regard as magic.

Brill and Barlow hate each other. Brill embarked on his search only because he was asked to do so by Barlow's wife Gloria, whom Jim loves. Barlow has no intention of returning home; instead, he is absorbing the personality of the legendary Genghis Khan, whose "thought-impressions" are preserved in a room sheathed with "psychic" metal from an ancient meteorite. By becoming Genghis in effect, he plans to conquer Asia with the initial help of the Mongolian bandit chief Togrukh Khan. He plans to buy the bandit's help by luring his wife to Khor and prostituting her to him.

Barlow schemes to reverse evolution and turn Brill into an ape, but before he can do so, he's stabbed to death by his mistress Lala Tzu, who feared that the scientist would cast her aside once he tricked Gloria into coming to Khor. As Togrukh Khan's raiders attack the city, Jim decimates them with a death-ray mounted on Barlow's palace. Although the folk of Khor invite him to become their new ruler, Brill prefers to return home to Gloria.

COMMENT

Although not great Howard, "King of the Forgotten People" is great fun nevertheless, from an era when Hollywood serials and B-movies cast all-American stalwarts as heroes of exotic adventures in distant realms that sometimes had science-fiction elements. In an alternate universe where Howard advanced quickly from the pulps to the bullpen of Monogram Studios in the mid-1930s, "King of the Forgotten People" might have become a chapter-play with John Wayne, Ray "Crash" Corrigan, or Bruce Bennett as Jim Brill, Preston Foster as Barlow, and as the seductive Lala Tzu...probably a western actress like Ann Dvorak cosmetized to look Asian in those more insular casting-call days.

Like "The Fire of Asshurbanipal," the story trims a typical Howard adventure story, Central Asian variety, with fantastic elements, in this case SF-style rather than full-on horror fantasy like the other. Whereas "The Fire of Asshurbanipal" started as a straight adventure that Howard later retrofitted with Cthulhoid elements, it's hard to tell if "King of the Forgotten People" underwent the same metamorphosis.

It would have been easy for the imaginative Howard to rewrite a colorful but essentially mundane "Oriental" adventure to include the genetically modified spiders that menace Brill in the opening scene, the unexplained "process of degeneration" with which Barlow threatens to de-evolve Brill, the scientist's "electric chain" that guards Khor from the Mongolian raiders, and the proto-laser beam that turns the attacking bandits into "a blackened mass of disintegrated flesh." It's equally plausible that he was trying to crack the science-fiction market at the outset, using a comfortably familiar setting from his El Borak adventures to help ease into a new market.

The strongest fantastic element in the story is the conceit of absorbing a dead man's personality so completely that one becomes the other person, even as to physical appearance. "You damned devil—*you're changing into a Mongol!*" Brill tells Barlow as he realizes that the scientist's physiology has begun to alter. One is reminded of the memoir by Howard's friend Novalyne Price Ellis, recalling a time when Howard discussed Genghis

Khan and seemed to move into the Mongol's skin. "Bob was not acting. He was there. At that moment, he *was* Jenghis Khan."

In a fantasy story, Barlow's transformation would be attributed to psychic possession or magic, but Howard attempts to give it a basis in pseudo-physics: "It's merely a matter of transmutation, of reduction to basic principles." Assuming that Howard tried to place the story with a science-fiction market in the first place, editors may have deemed that element too vague and far-fetched for their readers, although the science often was equally tenuous in other pulp SF of the time. Or perhaps, assuming it crossed his desk, an editor correctly surmised that the story was essentially a fast-action adventure with not enough integral "science" to qualify inarguably as science fiction.

"King of the Forgotten People" first appeared in *Magazine of Horror* in 1966 as "The Valley of the Lost" because of confusion over the title. It was mistakenly thought to be the story announced but never published by *Strange Tales* as "The Valley of the Lost." The error was corrected in later editions. It seems to be the kind of story that Howard might have hoped to place with *Argosy* magazine, whose mix of fiction included stories of the fantastic, or less ambitiously with *Astounding Stories*. Perhaps Howard or his agents had hoped to try Street & Smith's *Astounding* again after his success in placing El Borak and Kirby O'Donnell with the same company's *Top-Notch*. At any rate, the tale was welcomed posthumously by readers in 1966 who were pleased to see new material by Howard on the newsstands.

Available in *Adventures in Science Fantasy*.

People of the Black Coast
First published in *Spaceway Science Fiction*, September-October 1969

MAIN CHARACTERS
- Narrator
- Gloria
- Crab-people

THE PLOT

The narrator and his fiancée, Gloria, are stranded on a remote Pacific island after their private plane crashes en route from Manila to Guam. The island's black coast is composed of successively higher tiers of bare basaltic rock rising from the beach. As the two make do to survive, Gloria believes that something is trying to contact her through telepathy. Leaving Gloria on the beach, the narrator sets off to find a path up the cliffs. He comes across tracks in the sand that appear to be those of a crab, but if so, one as large as a horse.

Returning to the beach, he finds Gloria gone but makes a grim discovery of her severed hand. He passes out from stress and exhaustion, and when he wakes, he is surrounded by a throng of giant crabs with "keen, powerful brains." To their alien intellect, humans are no more than specimens to be studied—or a source of food to be eaten. Realizing that these beings killed Gloria, the narrator flies into a rage and tries to attack them. They hold him off with powerful "thought emanations" long enough to escape. And then the narrator begins a campaign of extermination, ambushing and killing the creatures with a makeshift iron bludgeon, as they respond with barrages of mental assaults. Even the loss of an arm, sheared off at the elbow by a dying foe, doesn't deter him.

As the narrative concludes, he plans to attack the crabs' city on the cliffs at dawn, when the creatures are "at a low ebb of vitality." He realizes he will not survive. "They took my mate; I take their lives."

COMMENT

"The People of the Black Coast" reworks elements from "The Children of the Night." In both stories, the protagonist suffers a shattering personal loss from inimical, inhuman foes. In return he sets out to annihilate his enemies even though he's fully aware that the war can only end in his own death. Regardless, he counts the cost worth it.

The plot is very slight, perhaps indicating that Howard thought that a shorter story would be more likely than a longer one to sell to an untried science-fiction market. We don't know the fate of the tale during Howard's lifetime.

Perhaps he decided—probably correctly—that *Astounding Stories* or *Wonder Stories* would find the concept of the intelligent crabs too sketchily developed, and more to the point, the plot too downbeat and violent for their audiences. So why waste the postage?

Even more to the point, perhaps, was the fact that Howard's central thesis ran counter, by and large, to the popular pulp science fiction of the time by Edward E. "Doc" Smith, Edmond Hamilton, and other writers. In "Doc" Smith's trend-setting SF of the 1920s and 1930s, human ingenuity unfailingly wins out over the aggressive impulses of alien species.

Howard takes a completely different tack. In a clash with an alien species, his narrator faces a challenge he's not likely to survive. His human intellect offers no advantage against another life form possessing the ability to weaponize telepathic powers. Worse, the other species is unable—or more likely, unwilling—to seek any sympathetic rapport with him:

> There was neither friendliness nor favor in their eyes, no sympathy or understanding—not even fear or hate ... these fiends gazed upon me in something of the manner in which cold-hearted scientists might look at a worm about to be stuck on a specimen board.

The story mentions one of Howard's close Texas friends when Gloria studies the black cliffs of the island and remarks, "Did you ever read Tevis Clyde Smith's poem—'the long black coasts of death'..." The reference is unlikely to mean much to casual readers who haven't heard of Smith. Perhaps Howard hoped that, if the story sold, the reference would open the door for his long-time friend as well.

But the story remained unsold during Howard's lifetime and saw print only much later in *Spaceway Science-Fiction*, edited by veteran editor and publisher William L. Crawford as a short-lived (1969–1970) revival of a magazine that Crawford had started in the 1950s. Fans may know the story best from dramatic cover paintings by Ken Kelly for the collections *Black Canaan* (Berkley Books, 1978) and *Beyond the Borders* (Baen Books, 1996; credited there to "C.W. Kelly"), in which it was reprinted.

Available in *Adventures in Science Fantasy*

Notes

- "The Challenge from Beyond" (*Fantasy Magazine*, September 1935) was a collaborative science-fiction fantasy by C.L. Moore, A. Merritt, H.P. Lovecraft, Robert E. Howard, and Frank Belknap Long. Howard wrote the fourth of the story's five chapters. In the preceding chapters, his colleagues developed the plot of an Earthman, George Campbell, who discovers a strange artifact in the Alaskan wilderness. In Lovecraft's chapter, the discovery precipitates an exchange of personalities between Campbell and a centipede-like alien. The story is usually classified as part of the Cthulhu Mythos because Lovecraft alludes to the *Eltdown Shards*, a Mythos text. Howard's chapter takes up the tale and provides names for the alien, Tothe, and his planet, Yakub. Lovecraft's chapter ended on a note of horror similar to that of his gothic story "The Outsider," as Campbell looks at his reflection in shock and sees "the loathsome, pale-grey bulk" of a centipede. Howard upends Lovecraft's revelation as Campbell recovers from his initial alarm and wonders, "Judged from a cosmic standpoint, why should his metamorphosis horrify him? Life and consciousness were the only realities in the universe. Form was unimportant." Once "doomed to live and die in his sordid niche as a human," he determines to seize the opportunity offered by his alien rebirth. "Not as a slave would he dwell on Yukub, but as a king! Just as of old barbarians had sat on the throne of lordly empires." He stakes his claim by disemboweling Yukub's "supreme lord of science," Yukth (as in *Almuric*, Howard seems fond of alien names that begin with "Y"), slaying a "worm-priest" in similar fashion, and seizing a mystic sphere that the alien folk worship as a god. Thus, he becomes "a Conan among centipedes," in L. Sprague deCamp's phrase. In Long's concluding chapter, Campbell-as-Tothe achieves his ambition on Yukub, but Campbell's body on Earth suffers a tragic fate, descending to mindless bestiality because "No spawn of Yekub can control the body of a human." It is available in *Adventures in Science Fantasy*.

- "The Gondarian Man" (*Fantasy Crossroads* No. 6, November 1975) is told in the form of a scientific report. Archaeologists exhume a large metallic capsule, from which a "hideous" creature emerges. The being slays four of the archeologists and then is slain in turn by a survivor wielding a ray gun. In a surprise ending, Howard reveals that the events take place "countless millions of years" in the future, the creature from the capsule is a human being, and the archaeologists are members of an altered future species. Howard envisions apocalyptic changes in biology and geology over the long span of the future, in terms similar to those used in his pseudo-essay "The Hyborian Age" to survey comparable processes back to the distant antediluvian ages of Kull and Conan: "Oceans rose and continents heaved up out of the deeps. Whole races died...mighty civilizations were lost." There isn't much to the story, but it's interesting to see Howard experiment—however tentatively—with the sort of visionary SF associated with H.G. Wells, Olaf Stapledon, and Arthur C. Clarke. It is available in *Adventures in Science Fantasy*.

- "The Supreme Moment" (*Crypt of Cthulhu* No. 25, September 1984) is an even slighter story. A fungus has begun to spread over the Earth, threatening human existence. The only hope is reclusive scientist Zan Uller, who has developed a way to destroy the fungus. He has never written down the formula, though. Approached for help by the wealthy and powerful, he notes his tormented life of early poverty, perpetual oppression, derision by men of science, and persecution by those of religion. "I owe nothing to the world." When the entreaties turn to a suggestion of physical persuasion, Uller commits suicide with a shot to the head. In its cynicism and pessimism, the story strays even further from the pulp SF formula. This is another story in which the protagonist's death from a self-inflicted gunshot to the head uneasily foreshadows Howard's suicide. It is available in *Adventures in Science Fantasy*.

Texas Terrors

Robert E. Howard experimented with settings in his own native region of Texas as early as 1928 with "Spanish Gold on Devil Horse," a colorful but non-fantastic adventure story about a hunt for lost treasure. It was set in "Lost Plains," a recognizably fictionalized version of his home town, Cross Plains. Curious readers can find it in *Post Oaks and Sand Roughs & Other Autobiographical Writings* (REH Foundation Press, 2019).

In the early 1930s, in correspondence with H.P. Lovecraft and August Derleth, he began to expound at length on the history, culture, and geography of Texas. With that inspiration, he started to use the state more and more as a setting for his weird fantasy work. Lovecraft later said he was "greatly pleased by [Howard's] recent tendency to employ his own southwestern background in fiction."

Howard's Texas Terrors include vampires, ghosts real and fabricated, Native American sorcery, deathless wizards in phantom cities, reincarnation, and bizarre cults invading rural west Texas from faraway lands. Of these tales, "The Horror from the Mount," "The Man on the Ground," and "For the Love of Barbara Allen" are ranked highly by fans.

I've omitted discussion of four stories with Texas settings from this section because they seem to fit better in other categories. "Marchers of Valhalla" begins in modern Texas and then becomes sword-and-sorcery as the inaugural story in Howard's series about James Allison, a modern Texan who remembers past incarnations as warriors in prehistoric eras that followed Conan's Hyborian Age. "Marchers of Valhalla" is surveyed as part of the James Allison series in Bob Weinberg's *The Annotated Guide to Robert E. Howard's Sword & Sorcery.*

"The Valley of the Lost" is discussed in my section on the Little People, given its affinity with that series. "Graveyard Rats" and "Black Wind Blowing" are surveyed under the Shudder Stories heading because they have traditionally been associated with Howard's fiction for the so-called "Shudder Pulps." For more information on the genesis of Howard's Texas stories, see *Western Weirdness and Voodoo Vengeance: An Informal Guide to Robert E. Howard's American Horrors* by the present writer (Pulp Hero Press, 2018).

The Horror from the Mound
First published in *Weird Tales*, May 1932

MAIN CHARACTERS
- Steve Brill
- Juan Lopez
- Don Santiago de Valdez

THE PLOT
Steve Brill, a young cowhand turned unsuccessful farmer, decides to explore a mysterious mound on his property, discounting a warning by his neighbor Lopez that a curse rests on the mound. He hopes that the mound might contain Spanish gold from the 1545 de Estrada expedition. Digging, he finds a slab of stone that covers a deeper opening. He goes to fetch a lantern as night falls, returns to find the stone displaced, and sees a shadow "slinking" in the direction of Lopez's hut.

A scream rings out, and Steve, investigating, finds Lopez dead with puncture marks in his throat. The Mexican was killed while writing a history of de Estrada's expedition. The de Estrada party was accompanied by Don Santiago de Valdez, a nobleman rescued from a deserted ship. The other explorers discovered that Valdez was a vampire as members of the expedition began to die, drained of blood. Valdez was buried in the mound while comatose, but with the removal of the stone, he has re-emerged. When he attacks Brill, the young Texan desperately fends him off, finally breaking his back and leaving him to be destroyed for good by a fire that consumes Lopez's hut.

COMMENT

"The Horror from the Mound" builds on a thesis that underlies several of Howard's weird fantasy tales about Texas:

> For some strange reason, the thought entered Brill's chaotic mind that though the land was new to the Anglo-Saxon, it was in reality very old. That broken and desecrated tomb was mute evidence that the land was ancient to man, and suddenly the night and the hills and the shadows bore on Brill with a sense of hideous antiquity. Here had long generations of men lived and died before Brill's ancestors ever heard of the land. In the night, in the shadows of this very creek, men had no doubt given up their ghosts in grisly ways.

Howard often used "hideous antiquity" or similar phrases in allusion to strange and often sinister secrets from forgotten ages of the past. In its appearance here, it suggests that the history of Texas is as long, mysterious, and haunted as the lost histories of Egypt and Mesopotamia, or the mythic Pre-Cataclysmic Age, and doubly ominous because the centuries before nineteenth-century settlement by English-speaking pioneers are often overlooked in the popular imagination.

Howard evokes the rich ethnic heritage of the state with the Scots-Irish-American Brill, the Mexican Juan Lopez, the Spanish explorers of Coronado's and de Soto's time, the ancient Mound Builders who were the predecessors or antecedents of the Indian tribes encountered by the first Europeans and Anglo-Americans, and an Afro-Caribbean slave who isn't named. The black man renders signal service by helping to find Santiago after his secret is revealed, and helping to bury him in the mound.

Don Santiago isn't the only vampire in Howard's body of work, but he's the closest to the model set by Bram Stoker's *Dracula*. Apparently an elegant and persuasive nobleman at the time he joined de Estrada's company, he's the worse for wear when he emerges after four hundred years in the ground:

> ...the tall, vulture-like form—the icy eyes, the long black fingernails—the moldering garb, hideously ancient—the long spurred boot—the slouch-hat with its crumbling feather—the flowing cloak that was falling to slow shreds. Framed in the black doorway crouched that abhorrent shape out of the

past, and Brill's brain reeled. A savage cold radiated from the figure—the scent of moldering clay and charnel-house refuse.

Howard's adjectives couldn't have been more perfectly chosen.

Brill faces the same dilemma that the Spanish explorers faced in their day: "human weapons were powerless—for may a man kill one already dead for long centuries...?" Bullets are useless against "the cold dead crawling thing." The Spaniards hesitated to apply the traditional method favored by Stoker's characters, that of pounding a stake through the vampire's heart and cutting off his head, for fear that Valdez would wake from his blood-sated stupor before they could finish.

Burying him under a massive stone in the mound was an expedient but ultimately futile solution. Here as in other stories by Howard, immolation is the only sure way to destroy a supernatural monster.

The tension is underscored and heightened by the realistic detail of the Texas milieu where economic survival rides on unpredictable and usually hostile weather conditions: "Plentiful rain in the winter—so rare in West Texas—had given promise of good crops. But as usual, things had happened. A late blizzard had destroyed all the budding fruit. The grain which had looked so promising was ripped to shreds and battered into the ground by terrific hailstorms just as it was turning yellow. A period of intense dryness, followed by another hailstorm, finished the corn." Howard offered similar observations in his letters: "In a life-time spent in the Southwest, I've seen perhaps a half-dozen full crops made. Drouth, floods, hail, sand-storms, boll-weevils, worms, grass-hoppers—all take their toll."

This is one of Howard's many stories, weird and otherwise, set in a completely masculine universe. There is no Mina Harker for Brill to save, Anglo or Hispanic, and no glamorous ladies in gowns with revealing necklines as in the Hammer Films vampire movies of the 1950s, '60s, and early '70s. However, with its tight plot and stark, windblown Texas setting, "The Horror from the Mound" doesn't really have any need or room for a love interest.

Available in The Horror Stories of Robert E. Howard

The Man on the Ground
First published in *Weird Tales*, July 1933

MAIN CHARACTERS

- Cal Reynolds
- Esau Brill

THE PLOT

A bitter feud between two cowboys, Cal Reynolds and Esau Brill, comes to a climax in the sun-scorched hills of west Texas. As he crouches behind a rock and snipes at Brill with his .30-30, while the other returns fire from his own cover, Reynolds determines to let nothing, not even death, stand in the way of his vengeance. After more than an hour of shots exchanged without any hits, Reynolds glimpses his enemy and fires, and hearing a cry of pain, raises his head inadvertently. Brill's rifle barks and Reynolds is dashed into unconsciousness. Recovering immediately, Reynolds finds himself lying in the open. Nearby lies his .30-30, barrel propped up against a stone.

Brill emerges from his cover, and Reynolds wildly breaks the paralysis that grips him and lunges for the rifle. He needs only to crook his finger around the trigger, as the muzzle already is slanted toward the other man. Brill strides forward leisurely, paying no attention to his foe but leering instead at the spot where Reynolds had been lying. Then Reynolds discharges his gun.

Shot through the chest, Brill topples over, an awful look of amazement frozen in his eyes.

As Reynolds rises, he notes that there are two corpses on the ground. A second body lies slumped among the rocks a few feet from Brill's body. Suddenly Reynolds realizes that he is gazing at his own corpse, shot through the head moments before. "And with the knowledge came true oblivion."

COMMENT

More a mood piece than a short story, "The Man on the Ground" is pared down to the bare minimum of action and detail, leaving nothing to distract the reader's attention from the atmosphere of tension and malevolence that Howard has carefully constructed. We are prepared for the shift from western melodrama to the supernatural ending early on:

> Unhampered by the stagnant and enervating shackles of sophistication and intellectuality, his [Reynolds'] instincts rose sheer from the naked primitive. And from them crystallized an almost tangible abstraction—a hate too strong for even death to destroy; a hate powerful enough to embody itself in itself, without the aid or the necessity of material substance.

Howard was a keen student of Texas feuds, waged in an environment where "geographical conditions and human temperament...were not conducive to long-drawn-out hostilities. There feuds were generally concluded with appalling suddenness and finality." The feud between Reynolds and Brill ends with similar jarring finality for the reader within the few thousand words of Howard's tightly constructed short story.

Of the no-quarter nature of the two men's mutual hostility, Howard says that "[a]fter a man has felt his adversary's knife grate against his bones, his adversary's thumb gouging at his eyes, his adversary's boot-heels stamped into his mouth, he is scarcely inclined to forgive and forget, regardless of the original merits of the argument." The rugged killing-ground of the heat-blistered hills is so vividly described that the reader can easily believe that this is a country that nurtures such all-consuming violence and monomania.

The ending has something of the unsettling, surrealistic mood of a bad dream as Reynolds sees the second corpse on the ground, with the homely detail of "a thin trickle of tobacco juice" oozing from the dead mouth, without immediately realizing what he's looking at. Then the ghastly knowledge follows: "He knew the feel of those shiny leather wrist-bands; he knew with fearful certainty whose hands had buckled that gun-belt; the tang of that tobacco juice was still on his palate." In its vivid accumulation of detail and the mordant impact of its stark conclusion, "The Man on the Ground" compares favorably with the classic American weird tales of Ambrose Bierce, a Howard favorite.

Available in The Horror Stories of Robert E. Howard

Old Garfield's Heart

First published in *Weird Tales*, December 1933

MAIN CHARACTERS

- Narrator
- Narrator's grandfather
- Jim Garfield
- Doc Blaine
- Joe Braxton
- Jack Kirby

THE PLOT

Old Jim Garfield has been badly injured while trying to break a wild pony. The narrator, a young friend of Garfield's, volunteers to accompany Doc Blaine to Garfield's ranch to help tend to the injured man. The narrator's grandfather, who has known Garfield since the frontier days, says that Old Jim has never seemed to age, remaining in appearance a man of about fifty.

Garfield is so badly injured that the doctor predicts he'll die before daybreak, but the old man says he can't die because he has the heart of an Indian god, placed there by a Lipan Apache medicine man, Ghost Man, after his own heart was pierced by a Comanche lance in a long-ago skirmish. "Only a bullet through the brain can kill me. And even then I wouldn't be rightly dead, as long as my heart beats in my breast." To humor him, Doc Blaine promises to remove the heart if he ever suffers a mortal head injury.

As Garfield recovers from his injuries, the narrator tangles with Jack Kirby, a local tough, and Kirby swears revenge. On a follow-up visit to Old Garfield with Doc Blaine, the narrator is nearly shot by Kirby in a ride-by attack. Instead, the bullet strikes Garfield, inflicting a massive, fatal head injury. Honoring his promise to Garfield, the doctor removes his heart from the corpse, and the narrator marvels: "In size and shape it was the duplicate of a human heart, but it was slick and smooth, and its crimson surface reflected the lamplight like a jewel more lambent than any ruby; and in my hand it still throbbed mightily, sending vibratory radiations of energy up my arm until my own heart seemed swelling and bursting in response."

An Indian warrior in traditional garb, Ghost Man silently appears at the door and extends his hand. The narrator proffers the heart, and as he departs and the other two follow, they see no sign of him—only something like an owl flying away in the moonlit sky.

COMMENT

"Old Garfield's Heart" is set in Lost Knob, Texas, a fictionalized version of Howard's own home town of Cross Plains. Jim Garfield is the embodiment of the old-time pioneers whom Howard idealized in his letters by type as "the old stock native Texan," and moreover, a symbol of the state's early Anglo history itself. Garfield claims to have fought in the Battle of San Jacinto in 1836, and to have saddled up with the iconic Texas heroes Ewen Cameron and Jack Hays.

"He tells some pretty tall tales," the narrator says skeptically. Here Howard kids the tradition of what Mark Twain called "stretchers" as a hallmark of American frontier humor, while slyly suggesting that not all such exaggerations should be completely discounted. The grandfather retorts that Old Jim was already settled in the area when he arrived in Texas in 1870. "He don't look a day older now than he did the first time I saw him." The evocation of Texas history and the story's true-to-life details of small-town rural life make it that much easier to ride along with Howard as he weaves his exotic elements into the plot.

Some of those fantasy elements reflect actual Native American traditions, such as the mystic power of the shaman and the respect given to owls as harbingers, messengers, or avatars of the spirit world. Howard's contribution to this mythology is the "heart of a god" given to Garfield by Ghost Man. With "its crimson surface that reflected the lamplight like a jewel more lambent than any ruby," it strongly resembles the Fire of Asshurbanipal, the Blood of Belshazzar, the Heart of Ahriman, and other fabulous gems in Howard's fiction.

Howard's spookily poetic genius permeates the story, as when Garfield remembers the night when Ghost Man brought him back from the dead: "All night Ghost Man did magic, callin' my ghost back from spirit-land. I remember that flight, a little. It was dark, and gray-like, and I drifted through gray mists and heard the dead wailin' past me in the mist." Like Old John Grimlan in "Dig Me No Grave," Old Jim Garfield has benefitted from a supernaturally extended life, but this time as a gift from a friend with mystic powers, not as the result of a deal with infernal forces on which the bill comes due with terrible consequences.

Available in *The Horror Stories of Robert E. Howard*

The Dead Remember

First published in *Argosy*, August 15, 1936

MAIN CHARACTERS

- Jim Gordon
- Old Joel
- Jezebel
- Joe Richards
- John Elston
- Mike O'Donnell
- Deputy Sam Grimes
- Tom Allison
- Coroner's Jury

THE PLOT

Jim Gordon, a young cowhand, stops by a cabin where Old Joel, a black man, and his mixed-race wife Jezebel live. In a drunken rage after losing at dice, he kills the couple. Before dying, Jezebel, who is regarded in the area as a witch, invokes the dreadful voodoo powers of "the big snake and the black swamp and the white cock." Gordon will be in hell before the year is out, and she herself will come to him "when the time's ripe," the witch swears.

Gordon joins a cattle drive to Kansas and becomes shunned by the other cowboys as a jinx when trouble plagues the journey. In Dodge City at the end of the drive, Gordon dreams of Jezebel appearing to him. He avers that as he cleans his pistol, his cloth has changed color from black and white to red and green, the same color as the dress that Jezebel wore when he killed her.

When Gordon is found dead at the back door of a saloon where he had been drinking heavily, a coroner's jury hears testimony from various witnesses including a teamster who says he encountered a mixed-race woman behind the saloon after he walked past Gordon sitting inside. She asked him to fetch Gordon outside, and the teamster says Gordon raced to the door and fired a shot, but the pistol burst in his hand. The jury reaches a verdict of accidental death from injuries inflicted by the explosion of the gun, the barrel of which had been stopped up by a piece of red and green cloth, evidently a rag from a woman's dress.

COMMENT

Could there be any better title than "The Dead Remember" for a story about retaliation from beyond the grave? This is another tale that enthusiasts now would classify as a "weird western." An 1877 cattle drive leads to Dodge City, and western icons Wyatt Earp and Bat Masterson are name-checked. Like the background elements of Howard's other tales of Texas Terror, these regional, historical details firmly ground in reality the grim account of supernatural revenge at the core of the plot.

Howard relates the story in a series of mundane documents: a letter from Jim Gordon to his brother that describes the murders of Joel and Jezebel, and leads up to the suggestion that Jezebel is about to make good on her pledge to pay Gordon back for murdering her and Old Joel; the accounts of the witnesses called by the coroner's jury; and finally the jury's report of findings. Howard experimented with a similar format in the "Pike Bearfield" burlesque westerns that he also sold to *Argosy* around the same time. Perhaps inspired by Mark Twain's and Ambrose Bierce's use of a similar device in their stories, this scheme further invites the reader to suspend disbelief in Jezebel's occult vengeance.

Jezebel's voodoo links the story with Howard's weird fantasy thrillers set in the Deep South. Those tales will be surveyed in the next section of this guide, Swampland Shadows.

As in "Black Canaan," a mixed-race voodoo witch has it in for a white, male protagonist. In "Black Canaan," the witch is a sensual, malicious vixen who luxuriates in exercising sexual and racial domination over the white protagonist. In "The Dead Remember," Jezebel persecutes Gordon for the simpler and more elemental motive of revenge for her murder and Joel's.

Black characters appear routinely in modern westerns, either as prominent supporting characters in novels like Larry McMurtry's *Lonesome Dove* (1985) or as protagonists, as in Joe R. Lansdale's *Paradise Sky* (2015). But they were mostly absent from westerns of Howard's time, or from mainstream fiction then as a whole, for that matter. When they did appear in movies or fiction by white writers, they were usually depicted as peripheral or subservient characters. In "The Dead Remember," Howard notably contravenes this formula. He depicts two strong minority characters who refuse to back down when insulted and abused by the drunken white cowhand, and he casts their plight in sympathetic terms as we read between the lines in Gordon's self-serving account.

"The Dead Remember" was reprinted for the first time in book form in *The Dark Man & Others* (Arkham House, 1963). Through an error in that edition, the story ended with the opening section, Gordon's letter to his brother. The documents relating to the coroner's inquest were unintentionally omitted. The full text has been restored in subsequent appearances in other collections and anthologies.

Available in *The Horror Stories of Robert E. Howard*

For the Love of Barbara Allen

First published in *The Magazine of Fantasy and Science Fiction*, August 1966

MAIN CHARACTERS

- John Grimes / Joel Grimes
- John's grandfather
- Rachel Ormond
- Doc Blaine
- Jim Ormond
- Bedford Forrest

- Confederate guerrillas
- Union soldiers

THE PLOT

A young Texan, John Grimes, listens to his grandfather sing the old folk ballad, "For the Love of Barbara Allen." The song reminds the old man that a neighbor, the elderly Rachel Ormond, is dying. Rachel was the sweetheart of the grandfather's brother, Joel Grimes, who often serenaded her with "Barbara Allen." As youths, Joel and his brother fought in the Civil War under the Confederate cavalry general Bedford Forrest. Joel was killed by a sharpshooter in one battle, and Rachel never married.

When one of his horses becomes restless in the barn, John leaves his grandfather to tend to the mustang. The horse rears and strikes John with its hoof, knocking the youth unconscious. Regaining his senses, John finds himself riding with a troop of gray-clad soldiers through hilly country. Led by a tall, saber-wielding commander, the company charges and overwhelms a convoy of troops in blue, the entire chain of events seeming like a vague memory to John.

At last, the youth comes face to face with a man whom he recognizes as his grandfather, but many years younger. "And in that flash, I *knew*." He stands, unable to move, as a bullet from an unseen rifleman crashes into his head. Waking again, he finds himself back in the corral, his head gashed where the horse kicked him. Realizing his "true cosmic identity," he races to the Ormond homestead, where the elderly woman recognizes him as Joel, and he sings "For the Love of Barbara Allen" to her as she passes away.

COMMENT

Unpublished until long after Howard's death, "For the Love of Barbara Allen" is rated now by many fans as one of his best stories, although it may not appeal to readers who prefer the testosterone charge of his sword-and-sorcery. The locality isn't specifically named, but the story clearly shares the "Lost Knob" setting of "Old Garfield's Heart"; the young Texan narrator (here named John Grimes), his grandfather, and Doc Blaine return.

The story reflects Howard's deep interest in American folk music, an interest that predated the popular folk-music revival of the 1950s and 1960s by three decades. He was particularly enamored of ballads from the British Isles that traveled to the early American colonies and became a part of Appalachian and Texas folk culture, like "For the Love of Barbara Allen." The character's ancestral history mirrors Howard's: both of his grandfathers saw service during the Civil War under Bedford Forrest.

As in "Old Garfield's Heart," vivid regional and historical details anchor the tale's fantastic elements in a realistic setting. As in many other Howard fantasies, reincarnation is a key component.

Readers accustomed to viewing Howard as a specialist in violent action will encounter him in a different mood here. The action is limited to a Civil War skirmish relived by the modern narrator in the last moments of his previous incarnation. The scene is related with Howard's usual verve as the narrator rides in a Confederate cavalry charge against a Union wagon train, but overall the work is wistfully tender in its mood. The story laments a tragically, prematurely ended romance, and excoriates the effects of war: "...it upsets the balance of things and throws lives into confusion that eternity can not make right."

Available in *Pictures in the Fire*

The Thunder Rider

First published in *Marchers of Valhalla*: Donald M. Grant, Publisher, 1972

MAIN CHARACTERS

- John Garfield / Iron Heart
- Conchita
- Tezcatlipoca, the Lord of the Mist
- Xototl
- Eagle Feather
- Conanche raiding party
- Pawnee warriors
- Guar the Northerner

THE PLOT

John Garfield, a modern man of Comanche Indian descent, is troubled by vague dreams of violence and war. Fearing that these unconscious desires and urges will end in violence, Garfield seeks help from an old medicine man, Eagle Feather. He learns that his visions are memories of past lives as Indian warriors. Through a grueling ritual that resembles but predates the Sun Dance of the Plains tribes, Garfield recalls a succession of past Comanche lives from the "immemorial past" up through the nineteenth century, including that of Iron Heart, the Thunder-Rider, the Scalp-Taker, a Comanche warrior of the 1500s.

In a sequence of adventures that Garfield now remembers, Iron Heart and his fellow Comanches wisely evade a larger party of enemy Tonkawas, clash with Pawnees led by the warrior-woman Conchita, and enter an eerie, misty land dominated by a stone fortress. Strange vibrations from a gong overcome Iron Heart, and he and the others are marched into the castle, encountering its ruler, Tezcatlipoca, the Lord of the Mist, a wizard. Iron Heart is thrown into a cell while the chamberlain of the castle, Xototl, tries to rape Conchita. She stabs him to death and frees Iron Heart, who confronts Tezcatlipoca and slays him with a curious axe found earlier with the body of Guar the Northerner, one of an assemblage of invaders who had entered the Plains centuries before. Thunder crashes, Iron Heart and Conchita flee the castle, and when the sun rises, mist and castle are gone. Iron Heart pledges to return to his tribe with the initially rebellious but finally compliant Pawnee warrior-woman as his wife.

COMMENT

Apparently dating from a few months before his death, "The Thunder-Rider" blends Howard's fondness for reincarnation with a Texas setting, although one from an era long before the Old West and twentieth-century backdrops of the tales previously surveyed. Where O'Donnel and O'Brien of the Little People series relived past existences as Celts, and James Allison remembered ancient lives of blond warriors in a mythic prehistoric time, John Garfield recalls past incarnations strictly of American Indian heritage.

Major elements in the story are drawn from REH's sword-and-sorcery fiction. There is a spirited woman warrior for the hero to fight, woo, and win; a lost city ruled by a sinister magician pre-dating even the Toltecs; a giant snake that the hero slays as he invades the villain's throne room; and a gong whose vibrations overwhelm Iron Heart with "the impact of a thunderbolt." The experienced Howard fan will have no trouble identifying antecedents. Nevertheless, placed in the fresh setting of the Texas plains in the days of the early Comanches, these elements showcase Howard's knack for recycling favorite motifs in different and clever ways.

In its present form, "The Thunder-Rider" suffers the shortcomings of a first draft that Howard may have filled out and polished had he enjoyed the opportunity. It is well-detailed and smoothly paced up to the appearance of Tezcatlipoca's castle. Then, as it hurries to a conclusion, it becomes more of an outline than a narrative. Even in this incomplete state, it provides enough action, color, and fantasy to warrant the reader's attention.

Available in *Western Tales*

Nekht Semerkeht

First published *The Black Stranger and Other American Tales*, University of Nebraska Press, 2005

MAIN CHARACTERS

- Hernando de Guzman
- Nekht Semerkeht
- Nezahualca
- Apache warrior

PLOT

Lost from the Coronado expedition to the Great Plains in 1541 in search of the Seven Cities of Cibola, a fabled realm of gold, Spanish conquistador Hernando de Guzman foils an ambush by a lone Apache warrior and then follows a hypnotic drum beat to a strange city in which a domed temple stands. A beautiful woman, Nezahualca, says that the city is called

Tlasceltec, and it's ruled by Nekht Semerkeht, a sorcerer from a distant land. Nezahualca says she is a Aztec princess by birth who was reduced to slavery by Nekht Semerkeht when she and her lover plotted to overthrow him.

She convinces de Guzman to enter the city and challenge the wizard. Once inside, the conquistador escapes a creature in the dark and saves Nezahualca from sacrifice to the Feeder from the Sky, a winged demon. He shoots Nekht Semerkeht but the sorcerer escapes. Claiming the city and Nezahualca as his own, the Spaniard sees Nekht Semerkeht in a dream in the likeness of an Indian. The wizard imparts a prophecy that he will return the city with an army of Comanches. The threat comes to pass, and de Guzman goes down fighting when the sorcerer and his Indian allies attack.

COMMENT

In a May 9, 1936, letter to August Derleth, Howard said, "I haven't written a weird story for nearly a year, though I've been contemplating one dealing with Coronado's expedition to the Staked Plains in 1541. A good theme if I can develop it." This seems to have been the inception of "Nekht Semerkeht."

It would be interesting to know whether or how the story was associated in Howard's mind with "The Thunder-Rider," another fantasy set centuries ago in Texas before Spanish and Anglo settlement. Both share certain elements of plot and theme, and both begin as relatively full narratives that dwindle down to outlines. Both, apparently, were begun by Howard shortly before his death, returning to action-packed weird fantasy after a hiatus of several months from the genre.

De Guzman is a fascinating creation, ruthless, ambitious, and daring—but despondent at the beginning of the story as he trudges through the southwestern desert, exhausted, without food, water, or hope of rejoining Coronado's band. His hopelessness leads him to question the very impulses that drive him forward. "He did not try to deceive himself into believing that there was any intellectual reason why he should not give up the agonizing struggle, place the muzzle of a pistol to his head and quit an existence whose savor had long ago become less than its pain." One is tempted to speculate whether we can read Howard's own mood into these reflections, not long before his own suicide.

"Nekht Semerkeht" sprints out of the gate quickly with an action scene—de Guzman's near scrape against an enterprising Apache—and then slows down for a fair amount of exposition before returning to stride when de Guzman meets the seductive but scheming Nezahualca. Howard would probably have smoothed out the rough edges in a second draft. As with "The Thunder-Rider," fans will be grateful to have the story in its present form anyway. The story originally appeared as a posthumous collaboration completed and partially revised by Andrew J. Offutt in *Swords Against Darkness*, a 1977 Zebra Books anthology. Howard's original draft was published in 2005 in the pure-text Howard collection, *The Black Stranger and Other American Tales*.

Available in *Pictures in the Fire*

Notes

- "A Horror in the Night" is a slight tale in which the young Texan narrator and his friend Bit Flynn decide to settle a difference with their fists. They start to have at it in a remote area on the border, but their slugfest is interrupted by the appearance of a violent lunatic with a knife. Before the psychopath can harm them, he steps on a rattlesnake. He tears the serpent apart before he dies from its bite. The basic set-up of the two young friends fighting is reminiscent of a scene from the fictionalized semi-autobiography *Post Oaks and Sand Roughs*, written in 1928, in which the narrator Steve Costigan remembers a spur-of-the-moment match against his friend Clive Hilton. "A Horror from the Night" may have been written around the same time. Unsold during Howard's lifetime, it appeared decades later in the journal *Cross Plains*, March 1974. It is available in *Sentiment: An Olio of Rarer Works*.

- "The Ivory Camel" is an unfinished thriller in which a young Texan, Karnes McHenry, kills a dark-skinned intruder in the family barn. A detective shows up later at the farm, after Karnes has reported the shooting to local authorities. The detective says the stranger was a fugitive of mixed Arab and Indian background who had murdered a cultist and stolen a jeweled Ivory Camel ornament from the sect. The fragment suggests that Howard would have woven a thriller in which the Texan tangles with the cult of the Ivory Camel, since Karnes has seemingly appropriated the missing relic. In autobiographical notes, Howard once claimed that "McHenry" was a family name later Anglicized as "Henry," brought to America by an immigrant named Shamus McHenry. The unfinished fragment was first published in *The Last of the Trunk*, Paradox Entertainment, 2007. It is available in *Tales of Weird Menace*.

Swampland Shadows

Howard's Texas Terrors were complemented by another series of regional weird fantasy stories set in the piney woods and swamps of the Deep South. H.P. Lovecraft thought highly of the Texan's ability to conjure "a clutchingly compelling picture of the horror that stalks through the moss-hung, shadow-cursed, serpent-riddled swamps of the American far south."

Howard's southern chillers can be sorted into two types—those in which the horror is indigenous to local culture, and those in which it intrudes from outside. The stories of the latter sort are surveyed later in this guide as Shudder Stories. The tales discussed here are rooted in regional voodoo practices and African-American beliefs, at least as those traditions were interpreted and dramatized by Howard. The Texan once said that he absorbed ghostly folklore as a child from two elderly ladies who had been born into slavery before Emancipation.

In a less fantastic and sadly more realistic sense, Howard's Swampland Shadows are cast by the tragic but inescapable history of black servitude in America. Although set after the end of the Civil War, the stories are haunted by racial fears and animosities that originated in the days when the practice of slavery shaped traditional southern culture.

The stories can be challenging for modern readers who come to them fresh, because they involve words and attitudes that still carry emotional and potentially hurtful connotations. In part, this content reflects Howard's attempt to portray his settings honestly and accurately, and in part it reflects attitudes that were closely ingrained in Howard himself and more generally in the American culture of his time, before the Civil Rights struggles of the 1950s and 1960s. In this sense, Howard was in the literary mainstream of the day, when authors routinely used words and perpetuated viewpoints that editors and readers today find offensive.

Some editors attempted to skirt this problem in the 1960s by rephrasing or finding euphemisms for Howard's terminology. Today's Howard enthusiasts prefer to restore the stories to their pure-text form, respecting the author's original composition while putting his content in proper cultural context. At that, Howard was far in advance of many other white writers of his time in creating strong, distinctive, often daunting and sometimes sympathetic black or mixed-race characters. In his stories of Swampland Shadows, it's these characters who shape the events of the plot. The white characters merely react.

Black Canaan

First published in *Weird Tales*, June 1936

MAIN CHARACTERS

- Kirby Buckner
- Saul Stark
- The Bride of Damballah
- Jim Braxton
- Esau McBride
- Tope Sorley
- Tunk Bixby
- Mrs. Richardson

THE PLOT

"Trouble on Tularoosa Creek!" The warning sends Kirby Buckner back home from the bustling streets of New Orleans to the backcountry of swamp-bordered Canaan. There, arriving by night, he encounters a beautiful, taunting, brown-complexioned woman on the lonely trail, and survives an ambush. Meeting up with his white neighbors from the town of Grimesville, he learns that a black man named Saul Stark has set up residence by the swamp, and "deviltry's bein' brewed up" in the black community there, descended from the slaves of antebellum days. Tope Sorley, a frightened black man, divulges that Stark is a voodoo priest or "conjure man" who plans to lead a war against the white population and "make himself king of Canaan." Any black people who resist his call are "put into the swamp."

Buckner rides out to warn the outlying white farmers, finds Stark's hut guarded by an invisible, hostile presence, and again encounters the seductive, derisive woman who says she serves the voodoo god Damballah. She places a spell on Buckner, which haunts him as he is joined by his friend Braxton and decides to locate and confront Stark. After Braxton fires at a shadowy form in the night, he's seized and killed by a figure that pulls him into the swampy creek. Buckner rides on alone to the House of Damballah, where Stark has gathered the black population for the Dance of the Skull performed by his consort, the Bride of Damballah who holds Kirby in her thrall.

The Bride intends to summon Buckner from his hiding place to his doom, but before she can do so, she falls dead from the bullet fired earlier by Braxton. Kirby confronts Stark and learns that the wizard, through some infernal process, has begun to transform his followers into inhuman, amphibian creatures, "dwellers in the swamp," who will help him over-throw the white population of Canaan. Braxton slays Stark in a herculean knife-fight. The shadow over the swamps is lifted.

COMMENT

Howard said that the setting of "Black Canaan" was drawn from "the real Canaan, which lies between Tulip Creek and the Ouchita River in southwestern Arkansas, the homeland of the Howards." Similarly, the daunting Saul Stark was inspired by the "sinister figure" of Kelly, a mysterious and widely feared conjure-man, whom tradition placed in the area. Howard wrote but failed to sell a supposedly true account of this figure, titled "Kelly the Conjure-Man."

The story's Damballah is an actual African-Caribbean-American voodoo deity, usually depicted in serpent form, whose frightful connotations in "Black Canaan" were con-sistent with white perceptions of voodoo in Howard's time. Modern studies paint a more respectful and positive picture of a belief system that combines traditional African beliefs with elements of Christianity. Saul Stark's monsters, who are subjected to his will and dreadfully transformed ("body... rounded and elongated,...legs dwarfed;...feet...flattened and broadened,...fingers horribly long, and *webbed*....expression... no more human than that of a great fish"), represent an ingenious idea by Howard to adopt, redefine, and freshen the traditional figure of the voodoo zombie.

With their fishlike appearance, amphibious nature, and nighttime sneaking-around, Stark's creatures are similar to H.P. Lovecraft's half-human creations in "The Shadow over Innsmouth." Lovecraft's beings are the offspring of matings between humans and an aquatic species. It's not clear whether Howard had read or knew of Lovecraft's story, which was written in 1931 but not widely published until 1942. Lovecraft thought highly of the "stark, living fear" that permeated "Black Canaan," but if he surmised any association with "The Shadow over Innsmouth," he seems never to have remarked on it.

Howard also employs sympathetic magic as a basic tenet of voodoo, when the Bride of Damballah tells Buckner that "by the blood in your veins I have snared you," using "seven drops of blood" from a scratch suffered in the ambush earlier in the story. But the enchantment seems as rawly, symbolically sexual as it is supernatural, when the reader views her attributes through Kirby's eyes: "...she was barbaric, in the open lure of her smile, in the gleam of her eyes, in the shameless posturing of her voluptuous body."

Although "Black Canaan" was included with other of Howard's best stories in the 1946 collection *Skull-Face & Others*, it went unreprinted after that until 1976. The late Glenn Lord speculated, I think correctly, that editors were wary of the story's racial implications in the sensitive era of the Civil Rights struggle. Since then it has appeared widely in collections and anthologies, where readers can evaluate it on its own terms, and perhaps even interpret it as a typically Howard-style sword-and-sorcery adventure in post-Civil War dress, especially when Buckner reflects that the Bride of Damballah's sinister Dance of the Skull "was ancient when the ocean drowned the black kings of Atlantis."

Available in The Horror Stories of Robert E. Howard

Pigeons from Hell

First published in *Weird Tales,* May 1938

MAIN CHARACTERS

- Griswell
- Sheriff Buckner
- John Branner
- Jacob Blount
- Celia Blassenville
- Joan (by reference)
- Blassenville sisters (by reference)

THE PLOT

Two travelers from New England, Griswell and Branner, happen upon a ruined plantation house in the piney woods of the Deep South. In the red light of sunset, pigeons fly from the dilapidated gallery. That night, as they camp out in the house, Griswell is awakened by an eerie whistling from upstairs. Branner mounts the steps as though in a trance, Griswell hears a scream, and then his friend returns wielding a hatchet, mobile even though his head has been split open.

Fleeing as he's pursued by a "wolf or dog, he could not tell which," Griswell encounters the county sheriff, Buckner. From the lawman, who goes back into the house with Griswell and finds Branner's body there, but determines from the evidence that he was killed by someone or something other than his friend, Griswell learns that the old house has a dark history. It was the ancestral home of the ruthless and long-departed Blassenville family, whose last mistress, Celia, was sadistically cruel to her mixed-race servant, Joan. Local black tradition holds that the souls of the hated Blassenvilles are released from hell at sunset as ghostly pigeons, and that they are only seen by someone doomed to die.

Strange things continue to transpire. Buckner and Griswell consult an elderly black man, Jacob Blount, who is reluctant to talk, fearful that the serpentine voodoo god will send "a little brother" with a white crescent on its head if he speaks too freely. But, rambling, he talks of Celia Blassenville and Joan, and says he once gave a woman a potion to create a "zuvembie," a transformed, undead human with supernatural powers whose "pleasure lies in the slaughter of human beings." Buckner tries to determine whether Joan used the potion to turn herself into a zuvembie to murder Celia, but the old man is suddenly struck and killed by a snake with a crescent marking on its head.

Now suspecting that the entity who killed Branner is the preternaturally powerful Joan, and that she still lurks in the house, Buckner returns there with Griswell as both men now see the ghostly pigeons fly away. After dark, Griswell hears the eerie whistling that previously summoned Branner, and unconsciously mounting the stair he sees something in the form of a woman, with a "face of horror" and a butcher knife. Buckner intervenes and shoots the creature. From an old portrait, the sheriff realizes that the zuvembie isn't the abused maid Joan, but the hideously, supernaturally transformed Celia Blassenville.

COMMENT

Like "'Black Canaan," "'Pigeons from Hell" had its origins in Howard family traditions. Robert told Lovecraft that as a child, he heard ghost tales from an elderly, mixed-race cook whom he called Aunt Mary Bohannon. In one tale, wanderers spending the night in a deserted old plantation house flee from a "monster" who comes downstairs in the dark, "sometimes armed with a broad-axe." Born into bondage, the elderly woman also "told tales of torture and unmistakable sadism" perpetrated on other female slaves by the white woman who owned her, Howard asserted. From his white grandmother, he added, he heard accounts of "the old, deserted plantation mansion, with the weeds growing rank about it and the ghostly pigeons flying up from the rails of the verandah."

The zuvembie seems to be Howard's own creation, another variation on the undead zombie of Haitian voodoo lore, different from but equally as creepy as Saul Stark's "dwellers in the swamp." The Big Serpent or Snake God feared by Jacob Blount corresponds to Damballah in "Black Canaan" and to the "big snake" that Jezebel invokes in "The Dead Remember."

Howard fans surmise that the Texan had his friend Lovecraft in mind in envisioning Griswell as a New Englander, especially when Griswell ruminates, "I could never think of black magic in connection with the South. To me witchcraft was always associated with old crooked streets in waterfront towns, overhung by gabled roofs that were old when they were hanging witches in Salem; dark musty alleys where black cats and other things might steal at night. Witchcraft always meant the old towns of New England, to me..." Playfully, he adds, "... but all this is more terrible than any New England legend..."— as if inviting Lovecraft to up the ante. But the story, written in 1934, went unpublished until two years after Howard's death and one year after Lovecraft's.

The main characters are well drawn, the unsuspecting Griswell contrasted with the experienced, authoritative Buckner. Some Howard enthusiasts note that the Texan's series characters Brule, Bran Mak Morn, and El Borak share common attributes of average but strong build, commanding personalities, and names that contain a "Br" sound. Sheriff Buckner, "a compactly-built man of medium height" and unassuming courage, can be added to that roster.

Although Conan the Cimmerian didn't make it onto film until 1982, "Pigeons from Hell" served as the basis for an episode of the television series *Thriller*, first broadcast June 6, 1961. Still available now on video, it was the first time that a new, post-pulp-era generation of fans would encounter Howard's work. The first book publication of the story followed in 1963, in the Arkham House collection *The Dark Man & Others*.

Available in *The Horror Stories of Robert E. Howard*

The Haunted Hut
First published in *Weirdbook* No. 2, 1969

MAIN CHARACTERS
- Ez
- Matapha'
- Aunt Sukie
- Two white hunters
- Unnamed black guide

THE PLOT
Aunt Sukie, an elderly black woman, tells a group of neighbors gathered at her cooking pot about Matapha', a red-eyed, cannibalistic spirit that lurks around a deserted hut in the nearby Hoodoo Swamp. Ez, a heavy drinker, expresses some skepticism at Aunt Sukie's story. He passes out from too much liquor and awakens to find himself in a dark, rundown cabin, which he realizes is the lair of the dreaded Matapha'.

He hears footsteps outside and sees two red eyes at the window—and then the story picks up the next day with two men on a hunting trip in the swamp. They find the hut and the remains of Ez inside. They conclude that he died from mundane causes and was partially eaten by hogs. But their black guide knows better: "Guess the wild hogs shut the door."

COMMENT
Unpublished and perhaps unpublishable during his lifetime, "The Haunted Hut" is an interesting experiment by Howard in writing a story through the viewpoint of an African-American character. The premise seems based on a thesis advanced by Howard in his essay "Kelly the Conjure-Man": "In every community of whites and blacks, at least in the South, a deep, dark current flows forever, out of sight of the whites who but dimly suspect its existence."

Or as Sheriff Buckner admits in "Pigeons from Hell," when confronted with the mysteries of Blassenville Manor: "The black people know more than we do about some things."

In "The Haunted Hut," the white population exemplified by the two peripheral white characters presumably knows little or nothing about the legend of Matapha'. Not so the black characters, who know and wisely fear the ghost or demon.

The plot itself is tenuously slight, designed to lead to the surprise ending where a common-sense conclusion reached by the two white men is undercut by the wiser, more observant black man employed as their hunting guide. The story may be best appreciated as an appendage to the richer, more fully developed imaginings of "Black Canaan" and "Pigeons from Hell."

Available in *Pictures in the Fire*

Skull-Face

The name Arthur Sarsfield Ward (1883–1959) is unlikely to resonate with many people today, other than veteran thriller enthusiasts who remember Ward under his once-celebrated pen-name "Sax Rohmer," creator of the fiendish criminal mastermind Fu Manchu. The first Fu Manchu novel appeared in 1912, and the series continued (with a fourteen-year hiatus between 1917 and 1931) until the author's death on 1959. In the U.S., the final two novels appeared as paperback originals under the famous Gold Medal label.

The popularity of Fu Manchu inspired several imitations, and decades later, after two world wars and the onset of the Cold War, Ian Fleming essayed his own take on the character with *Doctor No* (1958). In turn, in the wake of *Doctor No* and Fleming's other best-selling James Bond novels, Rohmer's novels enjoyed renewed popularity through new paperback reprints. Several Fu Manchu movies have been made, notably *The Mask of Fu Manchu* (1932) starring Boris Karloff and *The Face of Fu Manchu* (1965) with Christopher Lee.

Robert E. Howard expressed his own fascination with the character in an extravagant novella, "Skull-Face," serialized in three issues of *Weird Tales*. The work was immensely successful with *Weird Tales* readers, who had already taken note of Howard's growing mastery of adventure and fantasy with "Wolfshead," "Red Shadows," and "The Shadow Kingdom." When August Derleth assembled a substantial memorial volume of the Texan's work for Arkham House in 1946, he called it *Skull-Face and Others*.

Skull-Face

First published as a three-part serial in *Weird Tales*, October, November, and December 1929

MAIN CHARACTERS

- Stephen Costigan
- Kathulos of Atlantis
- Zuleika the Circassian
- John Gordon
- Yar Khan the Afghan
- Santiago the Haitian
- Kamonos the Levantine
- Yussef Ali the Moor
- Hassim the Senegalese
- Yun Shatu the Chinese
- Ganra Singh the Sikh
- Li Kung the Chinese
- Baron Rokoff
- Major Fairlan Morley
- Sir Haldred Frenton
- Police detectives
- Voodoo cultists

THE PLOT

Stephen Costigan, an American shattered physically and emotionally in the First World War, has become a drug addict who languishes in Yun Shatu's opium den in the London slums. He is plucked from the gutter by a mysterious figure known as the Master, who gives him an elixir to kill his craving for hashish and in return commands his obedience in murdering Sir Haldred Frenton, an adventurer and writer. For the first time, Costigan sees the Master's face: a fleshless living skull that he has glimpsed in opium visions. From Zuleika, the Master's beautiful slave, Costigan learns that their mysterious overlord is Kathulos of Egypt, a sorcerer and intriguer.

Costigan is intercepted by John Gordon, a government agent who has toiled unsuccessfully to infiltrate Kathulos' network of criminals, assassins, and spies, and quell the unrest that he has roiled in Africa, Asia, and the Middle East. The enigmatic mastermind plans nothing less than the creation of a "black empire" with himself as the ruler. After an unsuccessful raid on the criminal's lair, Gordon is kidnapped by Kathulos and almost sacrificed in a voodoo ceremony. Costigan intercedes, frees Gordon, and slays the swordsman Yar Khan and the voodoo priest Santiago before being overwhelmed by the cultists.

Regaining consciousness in a cage under Kathulos' scrutiny, Costigan learns that the skull-faced man is actually a survivor of lost Atlantis who was accidentally revived from eons of suspended animation when his watertight box was recovered from the sea. Then Gordon reappears and shoots Kathulos, who disappears through a secret door as Gordon and Costigan flee through an antediluvian network of underground corridors ahead of a charge of explosives that collapses the tunnels for good. Reunited with Zuleika, Costigan fears that he's dying as the last dose of Kathulos' elixir wears off, but instead he emerges from agonizing withdrawal, free from his drug addiction. As the world's authorities keep watch lest other horrors rise from the deeps, Costigan and Gordon fervently hope that "Kathulos was destroyed...when his world crashed about him."

COMMENT

By any measure of pulp excellence, "'Skull-Face" is a superb story of adventure, intrigue, and fantasy with a sure narrative pace. The action hardly flags, and even toward the middle as Howard necessarily spoons in more and more exposition between chases to build toward the final revelation about the Master's true identity, the reader is sped forward by the author's sheer creative energy and enthusiasm. Scenes such as the one in which Costigan grapples with the sword-wielding Yar Khan above London's nighttime skyline, "two human leopards, dope maniacs, [who] tore each other to pieces," rank with Howard's best blood-and-thunder writing.

As chapters headings for the story, Howard quotes appropriate excerpts of dark verse by G.K. Chesterton, Omar

Khayyam, Edgar Allan Poe, Algernon Swinburne, and other favorite poets. The practice bolsters the epic feel of the novella and places Howard in a line of succession from classic nineteenth-century authors who used the same device, notably Sir Walter Scott and James Fenimore Cooper.

The influence of Sax Rohmer is palpable, as John Gordon searches the dark byways of London's Limehouse district for a mastermind of "giant intellect and...monstrous genius" who engineers "a world-wide movement such as the world has never seen before." However, critics Richard A. Lupoff and Don Herron convincingly argue that the story rises above simple emulation and succeeds on its own merits because Howard put the stamp of his own personality on it. His investment extends to his first-person narrator's name, which was the same name that he gave to his fictionalized self in the autobiographical novel *Post Oaks and Sand Roughs*.

"As always the barbarian," Kathulos remarks of Costigan, reminding the reader that the story's bone-breaking action and ancient mysteries mark it as a uniquely Howardian sword-and-sorcery extravaganza in modern dress. 'Knives stung me and blackjacks smashed against me, but I laughed and drove my iron fists in straight, steam-hammer smashes that shattered flesh and bone," Costigan exults. At the same time, the American's drug addiction adds a new dimension of vulnerability to the Howard prototype of a hard-punching hero.

The novella shares a background of fabled Atlantis with other Howard stories of the time. Its suggestion of a world-girding civilization ruled by "mighty kings...many eons ago" corresponds to the remnants Solomon Kane discovers in Africa in "The Moon of Skulls." However, in that story, the Atlanteans are assumed to be of human origin, while in "Skull-Face," Howard suggests they were not only the creators of "a higher civilization of our own," but a different species. "No doubt we seemed as horrible to the Master as he did to us," Gordon remarks.

The question arises as the reader juxtaposes Kathulos' name with that of Lovecraft's ancient entity Cthulhu. Did Lovecraft's conception, set forth in "The Call of Cthulhu," published to acclaim in *Weird Tales* in February 1928, influence Howard's story, written that same year? One *Weird Tales* reader, praising Howard's story, asked about an "apparent connection" between the two shortly after "Skull-Face" was published. Howard himself said there was no association: "I merely manufactured the name [Kathulos] at random."

Howard student Patrice Louinet has noted that the name Kuthulos or Kathulos and the image of a skull-faced wizard appeared in an unpublished King Kull story written in early 1928. He suggests that Howard may have ported those elements over to "Skull-Face." That seems to be a valid thesis. Still, the parallels between "The Call of Cthulhu" and "Skull-Face" go beyond a mere similarity of names. Both stories are premised on the concept of an ancient entity who comes out of the sea, inspiring unrest among a disparate network of followers in what, in the 1920s, were the undeveloped and largely colonized areas of Africa, Asia, the Caribbean, and the Middle East. Without disputing Howard's response to the question, we may wonder whether, unconsciously, Lovecraft's story exerted an influence that Howard failed to recognize.

Available in *Tales of Weird Menace*

Taverel Manor
First published in *The Howard Reader* No. 8, 2003

MAIN CHARACTERS
- Stephen Costigan
- John Gordon
- Sir Haldred Taverel
- Lo Kung
- Marjory Harper
- Harry Harper
- Hanson
- Joan
- Thomas Hammerby
- Joseph Taverel
- Ali Massar

THE PLOT

Marjory Harper seeks John Gordon's help in locating her missing fiancée, Sir Haldred Taverel, who disappeared from his recently inherited manor on a remote English coast. Gordon agrees to look into it with Costigan, taking a hiatus from an inconclusive investigation into an opium-smuggling ring. The mansion is currently occupied by Hammerby, to whom the next-in-line for the Taverel estate, the wastrel Joseph Taverel, is in debt. Investigating a mysterious light shone from the manor, possibly as a signal to a foreign ship said to be lurking off shore, Gordon and Costigan are attacked in the fog by assailants. Costigan collars one—Ali Massar, a Malayan criminal who commits suicide before the two investigators can draw any information from him. Back in the house, Gordon and Costigan follow a cry for help into an underground passageway, where they are taunted by an elusively familiar voice and shot at by unseen gunmen. Presently they encounter Marjory Harper, her brother Harry, and her friend Joan. Harry says he was summoned to the manor by a note from Gordon. The detective responds that he never sent a note. An unfinished story by Howard, "Taverel Manor" ends there with several puzzles of the "old dark house" variety left unresolved and Skull-Face himself yet to appear—although it appears that the unseen observer who taunts Gordon and Costigan would have been revealed, at some later point in the story, as the Atlantean arch-villain.

COMMENT

A partially realized sequel to "Skull-Face," "Taverel Manor" begins somewhat as the earlier story did. In a dream—"or was it a dream"—a man experiences a frightful vision of being watched by someone or something with a grotesque face. But any strong association between the original and the sequel ends there. The narrative drive, bold vigor, and poetic imagery of "Skull-Face" are sadly absent from "Taverel Manor." The six completed chapters of the sequel lurch from one set of characters to another, establishing a set of mysterious events that never become very interesting in and of themselves.

The third-person narrative of the fragment shuffles Stephen Costigan from the center of the story, through whose viewpoint

"Skull-Face" was recounted, to a relatively subservient role as John Gordon's associate. "Silent, moody chap to those who don't know him," Gordon remarks. This taciturn, pipe-puffing Costigan is hardly recognizable as the broken, anguished figure who rose to heights of swashbuckling heroism in the earlier story. Gone too is the fantasy-tinged Atlantis mythos of the earlier story, replaced with the conventional props of a routine English drawing-room detective story, including a watchful Tibetan idol and three characters who may be something other than what they appear or profess to be.

From hints in Howard's letters to Lovecraft, "Taverel Manor" was a product of misfortune from the outset. Howard claimed that he initially abandoned the story for commercial reasons, once he learned that *Weird Tales* was going to move from a monthly to bi-monthly schedule and was going to stop using longer stories that would have to be published as serials. Later, when *Weird Tales* returned to a monthly schedule, Howard said he would "probably try" to proceed with the tale. Reading what remains of the story, one has the impression that Howard simply lost interest along the way, turning his energies instead to his sword-and-sorcery, sports, medieval adventure, and regional interests.

In 1977, FAX Collector's Editions published an illustrated hardcover edition of the story, completed by Richard A. Lupoff and retitled *The Return of Skull-Face*. As "Taverel Manor," this version was included in the 1978 Berkley Books paperback *Skull-Face*. Howard's original, unfinished version has since seen print.

Available in *Tales of Weird Menace*

The Noseless Horror
First published in *Magazine of Horror*, February 1970

MAIN CHARACTERS
- John Gordon
- Slade
- Sir Thomas Cameron
- Ganra Singh
- Gustave von Honmann

THE PLOT

Sir Thomas Cameron, a noted Egyptologist, invites his acquaintances John Gordon and Slade to his secluded estate. The two visitors are ushered in by Cameron's Sikh servant Ganra Singh, whose nose had been slashed off in a raid on the Afghan border years before, leaving his face grotesquely disfigured. Cameron displays an unusual mummy he claims to have found in Upper Egypt. He is guarding the thing carefully, fearful that other scientists will try to steal it. Gordon reminds his host that he, Cameron, also has been unscrupulous at times, having sent his rival Gustave von Honmann on a wild goose chase into Central Africa. There, von Honmann was murdered by a fiendish tribe, swearing vengeance against Cameron with his dying breath. According to reports, the corpse was withered by an unknown process, sealed in a chest, and left to adorn a fetish hut.

That night, the guests are awakened by a tumult from Cameron's study. Rushing in, they find the Egyptologist on the floor, a dagger in his chest. Dying, he reveals that he was attacked by "the noseless one." Suspicion falls on Ganra Singh, whom Gordon and Slade lock into a secure room. While Gordon prowls the study for clues, Slade leaves to examine other rooms in case the Sikh is innocent and the real murderer is still in the house. Among Cameron's curios, Slade finds a mummy case he believes contained the remains Sir Thomas mentioned earlier. The case is open, the mummy gone. In a nearby hall, Slade becomes aware of eyes gazing at him from behind a tapestry. A shadow is cast by something behind the hanging—a manlike, noseless shadow that sends Slade fleeing in panic.

The two men run the murderer to bay. It is Cameron's mummy, revived to fiendish and physically powerful life. The creature nearly kills Gordon before Ganra Singh appears and casts it into a roaring fireplace. Just before the flames consume the thing, the heat expands its withered face, and Gordon recognizes its features. The monster is Gustave von Honmann.

COMMENT

"The Noseless Horror" is the sequel to "Skull-Face" that Howard should have written instead of "Taverel Manor." Although not a sequel in the literal sense (and purists, therefore, may question its inclusion in this section), in mood and plot it replicates "Skull-Face" more faithfully than the true, unfinished continuation does.

As in "Skull-Face," a revenant that looks like a living mummy returns to exact revenge. In both stories, a brusque, straight-talking man named John Gordon, presumably of British nationality, figures as a major character. The Gordon in "The Noseless Horror" is a "wealthy sportsman," not a government agent with "a roving commission" like his namesake in "Skull-Face." Nevertheless, the two characters share the same blunt, impatient personality. The other Gordon could be substituted for this one with hardly any retooling needed.

In "Skull-Face," Kathulos evades the police by posing as an actual mummy. With some rewriting of the plot, he might have essayed the same subterfuge in "The Noseless Horror," infiltrating Cameron's manor house in a mummy case on some deadly mission of intrigue and assassination just as, in "Skull-Face," he waged a campaign of murder against various government operatives who threatened to expose his global conspiracy. Might Howard have conceived "The Noseless Horror" as a true follow-on with just this sort of scheme in mind, and then decided instead to write it as an unrelated weird fantasy? This is purest speculation, but the points of similarity certainly invite such a construction.

As it stands, "The Noseless Horror" holds up well as a story of the supernatural based on "the occult theory…that a spirit, earthbound through hate or love, can only do material good or evil when animating" a corporeal body. The murderous mummy with its "wrinkled leathery skin,…sunken cheeks,… flaring and withered nostrils from which the nose had decayed away; [and] hideous eyes…[that] burned with a ghastly and demoniac life," bears comparison with the great bandage-wrapped movie monsters of Boris Karloff, Christopher Lee, and Lon Chaney Jr.

Available in Tales of Weird Menace

De Montour

"I first became conscious of [Robert E. Howard] as a coming leader just a decade ago, when…I read *Wolfshead*," H.P. Lovecraft remarked to their mutual friend E. Hoffman Price in 1936, shortly after Howard's death. "I had read his two previous short tales with pleasure, but without especially noting the author. Now—in '26—I saw that [*Weird Tales*] had landed a big-timer of the CAS [Clark Ashton Smith] and EHP [E. Hoffman Price] calibre."

"Wolfshead" and its shorter predecessor "In the Forest of Villefère" were early attempts by Howard to merge sword-play and the supernatural in their depiction of melancholy Renaissance-era adventurer de Montour of Normandy, cursed with lycanthropy. The two-story series ranks with the other great werewolf tales of classic horror fiction, Jesse Douglas Kerruish's *The Undying Monster* (1922), Guy Endore's *The Werewolf of Paris* (1933), and James Blish's "There Shall Be No Darkness" (1950).

The setting of the stories is undefined, aside from details like musketry and the African slave trade that place it in the Age of Exploration. Several years ago, Howard enthusiast Edward Waterman speculated a time-range of anywhere from 1486 to 1520, based on the sparse internal evidence in the tales. That seems to be as good an estimate as any, short of simply locating the events in the freewheeling historical geography of Howard's vivid imagination.

Howard adds several fresh concepts to traditional werewolf lore, as noted in the comments below on the two stories. However, in "Wolfshead" at least, he adheres to the accepted fictional image of the werewolf himself as a tragic, haunted figure who is unable to control his feral instincts or to forget the havoc he causes in lupine form.

"My hands are red, my soul doomed to everlasting flames, my mind is torn with remorse for my crimes. And yet I can do nothing to help myself. Surely, Pierre," de Montour confesses to the narrator of "Wolfshead," "no man ever knew the hell that I have known."

In the fictionalized autobiography *Post Oaks and Sand Roughs*, "In the Forest of Villefère" appears as "The Road in the Forest" and "Wolfshead" as "Wolf Skull," both sold by Howard's alter-ego Steve Costigan to *Bizarre Stories* magazine. Informed that "Wolf Skull" will win the magazine's coveted cover illustration, Steve enthuses that he will "sure get a hand from the readers now—they always brag on the feature story." In fact, "Wolfshead" garnered the cover painting by E.M. Stevenson for the April 1926 issue of *Weird Tales*.

In the Forest of Villefère

First published in *Weird Tales*, August 1925

MAIN CHARACTERS

- De Montour
- Carolus le Loup

THE PLOT

While on a diplomatic mission, the French aristocrat de Montour of Normandy passes through the ill-reputed forest of Villefère in northern France. He encounters another traveller, Carolus le Loup, who offers to accompany him to the village of Villefère itself. Le Loup is an enigmatic stranger whose face is hidden from view by a mask. He speaks with a strange accent, slurring some words and apparently unable to.pronounce others. As darkness falls and the moon begins to rise, the two travellers discuss local legends of a werewolf said to haunt the area.

Just as the moon approaches its zenith, le Loup urges de Montour to pause at a small glade. The stranger seems to go mad, and performs a weird dance that he calls the "Dance of the Wolf." As he springs at de Montour, the Norman tears away his mask, revealing le Loup's face to be that of a wolf. De Montour and the werewolf struggle, and the nobleman injures the monster badly with a dagger. Knowing that he will be haunted forever by the werewolf's spirit if he kills the creature while it is partially in the form of a man, de Montour waits for the moon to reach its zenith and for le Loup to take on full wolf-form. Then he hacks the werewolf to pieces and flees.

COMMENT

More a vignette than a short story, "In the Forest of Villefère" was Howard's second published work of fiction. The work of a young writer flexing his creative muscles, it features no real plot, little complexity of interaction between the only two characters in the narrative, and the sketchiest of backgrounds. It is related in the first-person voice through the viewpoint of de Montour.

Even in embryonic form, Howard's narrative and descriptive skills are undeniably present, demanding the reader's attention at the outset:

> The sun had set. The great shadows came striding over the forest. In the weird twilight of a late summer day, I saw the path ahead glide on among the mighty trees and disappear. And I shuddered and glanced fearfully over my shoulder. Miles behind lay the nearest village—miles ahead the next.

Howard builds tension admirably as the tale progresses. Le Loup's first appearance, "a tall, thin man, vague in the twilight," is impressive, as is de Montour's discovery that the stranger wears a mask—as a religious vow, signifying thanks for divine help in escaping a pack of hounds, le Loup implies. Le Loup's difficulty in pronouncing certain words is a clever detail, consistent with the notion that someone with the face of a wolf would find it difficult to articulate certain sounds. It's a creative departure, too, from the routine portrayal of a werewolf as a snarling, inarticulate creature.

Howard's innovative contribution to werewolf lore proposes that "if a werewolf is slain while a wolf, then he is slain, but if he is slain as a man, then his half-soul will haunt his slayer forever." Thus, it seems, lycanthropy is a matter of demonic possession, rather than the result of an infection passed on to the victim from the werewolf's bite, as we usually see in horror movies.

This conceit tightens the tension as well. De Montour is torn between the fear of delaying a fatal blow to le Loup, lest the creature rally from its injuries, and the dread of becoming a werewolf himself if he strikes too soon. In style and creative thought, the short tale clearly foreshadows the strengths that characterize Howard's mature works of weird fantasy.

Available in The Horror Stories of Robert E. Howard

Wolfshead

First published in *Weird Tales*, April 1926

MAIN CHARACTERS

- Pierre (the narrator)
- de Montour
- Dom Vincente da Lusto
- Ysabel da Lusto
- Carlos
- Marcita Verenza
- Luigi Verenza
- Jean Desmarte
- Baron von Schiller
- Don Florenzo de Seville
- Gola

THE PLOT

Several noblemen and adventurers have been invited to the castle of their mutual friend, the wealthy trader Dom Vincente da Lusto, on the west coast of Africa. The most unusual of these guests is de Montour, a taciturn Frenchman, who warns the narrator, Pierre, on Pierre's first night in the castle, to bar and bolt the door to his room before going to bed. Pierre does so, and hears something pulling and shoving against the bolted door later that night.

The next day, Dom Vincente and his guests learn that a native in a nearby village was torn to pieces by a savage beast during the night. The beautiful Marcita Verenza tells Pierre that de Montour also had warned her the previous evening to bar her door, and that she was later awakened by something fumbling at the door. Displaying a dagger, Marcita promises to keep her room unlocked that night to "see whom I catch."

Later, two other guests, Baron von Schiller and Jean Desmarte, cross swords in their rivalry for Marcita's affections. Their duel is brought to a quick halt by Marcita's brother Luigi.

That night, something invades Marcita's room and attacks her. The German von Schiller is found dead elsewhere in the castle. Suspicion for the crimes falls on the German's rival Desmarte, but de Montour points out that von Schiller was slain by the claws of a wild beast. When more tribesmen are killed in a nearby village, the villagers believe that the murderer is Dom Vincente. The next night, encountering de Montour in a hallway, Pierre witnesses the appearance of a vague form that merges with the other man, whereupon de Montour's face takes on "a hideous, a bestial" appearance. Pierre escapes the creature, learning subsequently that de Montour was cursed with lycanthropy after his encounter with the werewolf in the forest of Villefère. He had slain the creature before it turned fully into a wolf, thereby inheriting its evil spirit.

Tensions mount. Pierre learns that Dom Vincente's wastrel nephew Carlos plans to sell his uncle into the hands of the villagers and to incite the murder of the other guests. When the tribesmen unite with other warriors along the coast to storm the castle, de Montour volunteers to swim the river and set off the powder stored in a warehouse, with the intent of foiling the attack. The tactic is successful, but Pierre becomes lost in the jungle after taking part in a sortie against the retreating warriors. Eventually, he comes upon a lonely hut, and inside the hut is de Montour. The aristocrat says that the evil spirit of the werewolf fled his body during the ordeal of his swim across the river. He is a free man once more.

COMMENT

"Wolfshead" shows considerable advancement from "In the Forest of Villefère" with a longer and more lavish plot, an extensive cast of colorful characters, and plentiful, well-written dialogue flavored lavishly but not overwhelmingly with the sort of archaic language that readers in Howard's day, at least, expected from stories in the vein of Alexander Dumas and Rafael Sabatini.

Although not the protagonist, de Montour is clearly the pivotal character of the tale, commanding the narrator's curiosity from the outset: "...it was neither his clothes nor his sword which attracted my attention. It was his face. A refined, high-bred face, it was furrowed deep with lines that gave it a weary, haggard expression. Tiny scars flecked jaw and forehead as if torn by savage claws; I could have sworn the narrow gray eyes had a fleeting, haunted look in their expression at times."

Howard expands ingeniously upon the lycanthropy lore introduced in the earlier story:

> In the beginning, the world was strange, misshapen. Grotesque beasts wandered through its jungles. Driven from another world, ancient demons and fiends came in great numbers and settled upon this newer, younger world. Long the forces of good and evil warred.
>
> A strange beast, known as man, wandered among the other beasts, and since good or bad must have a concrete form ere either accomplishes its desire, the spirits of good entered man. The fiends entered other beasts, reptiles and birds; and long and fiercely waged the age-old battle. But man conquered. The great dragons and serpents were slain and with them the demons. Finally, Solomon, wise beyond the ken of man, made great war upon them, and by virtue of his wisdom, slew, seized and bound. But there were some which were the fiercest, the boldest, and though Solomon drove them out he could not conquer them. Those had taken the form of wolves. As the ages passed, wolf and demon became merged. No longer could the fiend leave the body of the wolf at will. In many instances, the savagery of the wolf overcame the subtlety of the demon and enslaved him, so the wolf became again only a beast, a fierce, cunning beast, but merely a beast. But of the werewolves, there are many, even yet.
>
> And during the time of the full moon, the wolf may take the form, or the half-form of a man. When the moon hovers at her zenith, however, the wolf-spirit again takes ascendency and the werewolf becomes a true wolf once more. But if it is slain in the form of a man, then the spirit is free to haunt its slayer through the ages.

This passage recalls the mythologies that underpin certain other stories by Howard. In the Solomon Kane fantasy "The

Footfalls Within," an Arabian *hadji* speaks of Solomon as Suleiman ben Daoud, who "drove forth the conjurers and magicians and prisoned the efreets and the evil genii!" "The great dragons" re-enter the Howard universe in "The Valley of the Worm" and "Red Nails." The reference to the "fiends [who] entered other beasts, reptiles and birds" recalls the primeval war described in "The Shadow Kingdom," in which early humankind fought and dispersed "the bird-women, the harpies, the bat-men, the flying fiends, the wolf-people, the demons, the goblins...and...the wolf-men." Once Howard seized upon a novel concept, he rarely discarded it after only one use. At that, the image of a demon-haunted stronghold on a remote coast, besieged by hostile indigenous warriors, would appear again in "The Black Stranger," one of the last Conan adventures.

The title "Wolfshead" serves a double purpose. In its olden meaning as a term for an outlaw or masterless adventurer, it appropriately defines de Montour's situation as a wandering, bloodstained outcast. More to the point of Howard's werewolf mythology, it refers to the omen that appears as de Montour's demonic spirit prepares to invade and transform his body: "On the wall behind de Montour appeared a shadow, a shadow clearly defined of a *wolf's head!*"

Howard returned to the werewolf theme in two other stories unrelated to the de Montour diptych, "The Hyena" and "Black Hound of Death." Each treated the concept in new and different ways. The former is addressed below in the section on Howard's Jungle Horrors, and the second in the later section on Shudder Stories.

Available in *The Horror Stories of Robert E. Howard*

Jungle Horrors

In a 1930 letter to H.P. Lovecraft, Robert E. Howard wrote tremulously of "the sullen, dank, devil-haunted swamps of the [African] Slave Coast with its abhorrent secrets, night-black jungles, squalling teeming life, where fires flared and tom-toms thundered through the thick, musky night and black naked figures leaped and howled before blood-stained idols."

Lest anyone take offense at this portrait of unclothed, primitive Africans engaged in possibly orgiastic rites, let's remember that most Americans some ninety years ago knew little more about Africa than the hokum they saw in the simple-minded jungle movies of the time. Even H. Rider Haggard, who had actually resided in Africa for a time as a British colonial employee in the Transvaal, painted the continent in broad, romantic strokes in his fiction.

Howard was better read than most of his contemporaries in the general public. From one of the late Harold Preece's memoirs, we know that Howard had read *The Story of an African Farm* (1883), a realistic, semi-autobiographical novel by Olive Schreiner set in the semi-arid Karoo region of South Africa. Some of Schreiner's workaday details about rural colonial life in Africa seem to be reflected in the setting of "The Hyena," one of Howard's African weird fantasy stories. But Howard was less interested in the realities of Africa than in its potential as a backdrop on which to superimpose stories of mayhem and the supernatural, heated to fever pitch by sweltering tropical temperatures.

Commercially, Howard's most successful ventures into the jungle were "Wolfshead," previously discussed, and four masterpieces in the Solomon Kane series—"Red Shadows," "The Moon of Skulls," "The Hills of the Dead," and "Wings in the Night." The Solomon Kane series was surveyed by Robert Weinberg in *The Annotated Guide to Robert E. Howard's Sword & Sorcery.* The Texas writer had mixed success with his non-series efforts. Three appeared in *Weird Tales* and its short-lived sibling, *Oriental Stories.* Others went unsold during his lifetime and saw print only decades after his death.

The Dream Snake

First published in *Weird Tales*, February 1928

MAIN CHARACTERS

- Unnamed narrator
- Faming
- Other guests or residents at a bungalow

THE PLOT

The narrator and Faming are among several people assembled on the veranda of a bungalow as a breeze ripples the grassy lawn, startling Faming. Faming relates a lifelong dream in which he owns an estate in Africa. Returning from a hunting trip with a broken rifle, the dream-Faming finds a track of crushed grass leading to his house. Inside, furniture is overturned and broken, and a Hindu servant is missing. In the dream, Faming realizes that the mayhem has been wrought by a gigantic serpent, which might still be lurking in the high grass.

The dream-Faming locks himself in the house, as something slithers audibly through the grass outside. At times the door bulges inward as a heavy weight presses against it, until day breaks, the disturbance ends, and the dream-Faming flees, hoping to escape the grasslands before the next sunset. But he is still trapped in the tall grass as night falls again, and he sees the grass part behind him with the slithering of the monstrous constrictor, approaching ever closer with each dream. He always wakes at this juncture, fearful of his fate if the dream snake ever reaches him. That night, the narrator and the others are wakened by wild laughter and a final scream from Faming's room. Faming is dead on the floor. There is no mark on the corpse, but Faming's face is distorted as if he had been crushed by a terrific force, like the embrace of a great constrictor.

COMMENT

"The Dream Snake" was one of three minor but respectably dark and imaginative horror stories by Howard published in *Weird Tales* in 1928, just before the debut of Solomon Kane with "Red Shadows" in the August issue. Faming's obsessive dream about the unseen but deadly serpent is skillfully developed. Like "The Touch of Death" surveyed in the section on Howard's ghost stories, the story calls to mind Ambrose Bierce's mordant tales of psychological horror.

The story is effective in part because it draws upon three elements of Howard's own personality: his loathing of snakes, his troubled sleep patterns as a child and young man, and his interest in the dream state. Howard often commented on his own vivid dreams of being someone else. In at least one instance described to Lovecraft, Howard's dream-self perceived Howard's actual waking life as a dream. In his sword-and-sorcery and weird fantasy tales in which modern men remember past incarnations in states of unconsciousness and semi-consciousness, Howard takes this concept of dream-otherness in a different and more extravagant direction.

Available in *The Horror Stories of Robert E. Howard*

The Hyena

First published in *Weird Tales*, March 1928

MAIN CHARACTERS

- Steve, the narrator
- Senecoza
- Ellen Farel
- Ludtvik Strolvaus
- Senecoza's warriors

THE PLOT

While staying at his distant cousin Ludtvik's cattle ranch on the east coast of Africa, an American from Virginia, Steve, nurses an

instinctive hatred for Senecoza, a Masai witch-doctor. Senecoza
is associated in some obscure way with the murder of a chief
who was killed by hyenas. Steve senses that the witch-doctor or
fetish-man returns his enmity, and plans to kill him. When he
sees Senecoza gazing with "serpentlike eyes" at another vacationing American, Ellen Farel, Steve raises his gun to shoot him.
But Senecoza looks at him, and he is unable to pull the trigger.

Violent incidents follow. A hyena attacks Steve, but the
American escapes without serious harm. Then after an
assault by Senecoza and twenty warriors, Steve learns that
the witch-doctor plans to exterminate all the white settlers in
the area. After warning his neighbors that an attack is immi-
nent and then rescuing Ellen from Senecoza, Steve squares off
with the fetish-man. Senecoza hides in tall grass, from which
emerges the hyena who attacked the American earlier. Steve
mortally wounds the beast, which escapes to Senecoza's hut.
Inside, Steve and other settlers find no hyena. But Senecoza is
there, dead from Steve's bullet.

COMMENT

Although the first-person narrator of "The Hyena," Steve,
is never given a last name, readers may surmise that this is
another Steve or Stephen Costigan, given how often Howard
used that name for the protagonists in his stories from 1928
and 1929. However, this Steve comes from Virginia, not Texas
as one might have expected.

This story foreshadows Howard's later tales of racially
themed sorcery and skullduggery pitting a white protagonist against a black antagonist in the American Deep South.
Specifically, the opposing figures of Steve and Senecoza parallel those of Kirby Buckner and Saul Stark in "Black Canaan."
When Steve rides to warn neighboring ranchers of the Masai
uprising fomented by the witch-doctor, the reader is likely to
remember Buckner's dash to warn his neighbors about the
uprising instigated by Stark.

On the surface, by substituting an African backdrop for an
American one, "The Hyena" would seem less likely than "Black
Canaan" to provoke the racial sensitivities of modern readers
in the post-Civil Rights era. However, when Steve takes offense

at what he interprets as Senacoza's sexual interest in Ellen, and says, "It seemed to me...incredible that a black man, no matter what his rank, should look at a white woman as he did," it seems immaterial whether the setting is Africa or Black Canaan. Either way, it's an attitude that is likely to grate on readers today. In the context of the times in which Howard wrote, it would have been viewed much differently by the average white reader.

At least Howard is honest in identifying the basic nature of Steve's hatred toward Senecoza: "Because I came from Virginia, race instinct and prejudice were strong in me, and doubtless the feeling of inferiority which Senecoza constantly inspired in me had a great deal to do with my antipathy for him." And an admission that carries an element of truth, perhaps uncomfortably so for white readers, even today: "I always had a vague feeling that the black was mocking us."

In the structure of the plot, Steve attitude is mitigated by the fact that the witch-doctor returns his hostility. Senecoza is sufficiently practiced in masking his intentions that the other white characters fail to recognize the threat he poses. It is notable that the black man emerges as a stronger, more memorable figure than the unpolished narrator or his "winsome" love interest, Ellen. Ellen is typical of the women in Howard's early stories who exist only as someone for the hero to rescue. Howard's women who stand on their own two feet—Red Sonya, Dark Agnes, and the like—were yet to be realized.

How does Senecoza transform himself into a hyena? Howard never explains, and for the purposes of the story, he doesn't need to, leaving it vaguely as an aspect of the fetishman's magical powers.

Available in The Horror Stories of Robert E. Howard

The Voice of El-Lil

First published in *Oriental Stories*, October-November 1930

MAIN CHARACTERS

- Bill Kirby
- John Conrad
- Naluna

- Sostoras
- Gorat
- Selim
- Sumerians

THE PLOT

In the Middle Eastern port of Maskat, a traveler is surprised when the man at the next table, Bill Kirby, jumps at the sound of a miniature gong. Kirby, a veteran hunter and adventurer, recounts his story of meeting up once with John Conrad, a young professor from New England. The two men journeyed into a distant area of Somaliland on which "a mighty ju-ju curse" was said to rest. An odd sound in the night, "deep, vibrant, melodious," caused all but one of their servants to desert. Attacked by armed raiders in strange garb, Kirby and Conrad were taken to a walled city, Eridu, on a remote lake. In the midst of the city was a structure that resembled the Biblical Tower of Babel. This was the temple of the god El-lil, whose "voice" was personified in the vibrations from a gong in the tower. The residents of the city were descended from Sumerians who fled the destruction of their home kingdom thousands of years before.

Tied up before the gong, the two adventurers were nearly driven mad by its vibrations until they were freed by Naluna, a dancing girl, with whom Conrad was smitten. Escaping across the lake, they fought off pursuing soldiers. Naluna was mortally wounded, but she told the grieving Conrad that they were lovers in past lives, and would meet again in future incarnations. The Voice of El-lil followed the fugitives through the jungle, hypnotically compelling Conrad to return, but Kirby knocked his friend unconscious before he could comply, and they eventually reached safety. "[I]f you don't believe me, I won't blame you at all," Kirby tells his listener, who elects to accept the story.

COMMENT

An amazing feat of narrative imagination, "The Voice of El-lil" draws inspiration from *Allan Quatermain* (1887) and other novels by H. Rider Haggard about lost civilizations in modern Africa, but Howard goes Haggard one better. Where Haggard customarily spun out his tales over the course of 300 or more pages, Howard compresses his story into less than a tenth of that number of pages.

Once past the framing device in Maskat, the story moves at a speedy clip, with a short pause in the middle—once Kirby and Conrad are imprisoned in Eridu—for Howard to spoon in several paragraphs of exposition about the history of Sumer, the decay or retrogression of civilizations into barbarism, and the ethnic origins of the original Sumerians. Even the exposition draws the reader along on the wings of Howard's exuberance in discussing some of his favorite topics.

Conan fans are likely to focus on the tale's violent action scenes, described with Howard's characteristic verve:

> He sprang in like a blood-mad tiger, hacking for my head. I ducked and avoided the full force of the blow but couldn't get away from it altogether and it laid my scalp open in a three-inch gash, clear to the bone. ... I felt [my] ax crunch through metal and bone, the haft splintered in my hand, and there was Gorat dead at my feet in a horrid welter of blood and brains.

Enthusiasts of fiction about exotic lost ages may prefer, instead, the story's poetic prose depicting the voice of El-lil:

> I knew Naluna was right when she told us that her ancestors brought [the gong] with them on that long, grueling trek, ages ago, when they fled before Sargon's wild riders. And how many eons before that dim time must it have hung in El-Lil's temple in Nippur, Erech, or Old Eridu, booming out its mellow threat or promise over the dreamy valley of the Euphrates, or across the green foam of the Persian Gulf.

But the typical hardcore Howard fan, who generally enjoys the full range of the author's surging imagination, will luxuriate in the full package. The tale doesn't skimp either on the darkly fantastic element of the gong and the supernaturally mesmeric power of its call:

> I never saw or heard of a gong before or since whose notes could convey so many different meanings. This was an insidious call—a luring urge, yet a peremptory command for us to return. It threatened and promised; if its attraction had been great before we stood on the tower of El-lil and felt its full power, now it was almost irresistible. It was hypnotic. I know

now how a bird feels when charmed by a snake and how the snake himself feels when the fakirs play on their pipes.

The reader will be reminded of other weird fantasy works by Howard in which a character is lured irresistibly to certain doom by a hypnotic sound or spell. How did Howard and the editors justify including a story about Africa in a magazine titled *Oriental Stories*? Howard offers an association in passing, as Kirby says of their captors:

> They had the look of the Orient about them but not the Orient with which I was familiar, if you understand me. Africa is of the East but not one with it. They looked no more African than a Chinaman does. This is hard to explain. But I'll say this: Tokyo is Eastern, and Benares is equally so, but Benares symbolizes a different, older phase of the Orient, while Peking represents still another, and older one. These men were of an Orient I had never known; they were part of an East older than Persia—older than Assyria—older than Babylon!

It still seems a stretch, but a good story is a good story.

"The Voice of El-lil" is another Howard tale that exists in at least two versions because of editorial emendation (or intrusion) over the course of nearly ninety years. When it was reprinted in *The Avon Fantasy Reader* in 1950 as "The Temptress of the Tower of Torture and Sin," the editors were evidently disturbed by the racial implications of a sentence that glorified Kirby as a specimen of "the original Anglo-Saxon stock." Instead, they substituted a different phrase, "the original barbarian stock," perhaps with an eye for reminding readers that this was the same writer who had created Conan.

Likewise, at the end, where Howard's original text celebrated Kirby as "a true brother of the roving, fighting, adventuring Sons of Aryan," the reprint instead described him as "a true brother of the roving, fighting, adventuring Sons of Man." Another corruption: Howard's original opening location of Maskat (Mascat in modern iteration) was misspelled along the way as Muskat. This lightly but implacably bowdlerized version persisted through several hardcover and paperback collections, even into the Baen Books softcover editions of the 1990s. More recent editions have restored the pure text.

Available in Pictures in the Fire

The Cobra in the Dream
First published in *Weirdbook* No. 1, 1968

MAIN CHARACTERS
- Costigan
- John Murken
- Hindu outlaws

PLOT
Adventurer John Murken is afraid to fall asleep and dream. He tells his friend Costigan that several years before, in India, searching for the fabled treasure of Alam Singh, he was captured by Hindu outlaws who guarded the hoard. They subjected him to a fiendish torture, staking him down in a cave, near a cobra that was restrained from biting him only by a single rawhide cord. Water was left to drip on the cord, the moisture allowing the hide to stretch and enabling the serpent to draw nearer and nearer to the captive. An oil lamp provided the only light, and Murken feared that it would go out and the cobra would administer its fatal bite in the darkness. Although he was rescued by hunters before the cobra could reach him, he continues to relive the ordeal in a persistent dream. He anticipates that, in the next dream, the light will go out, the snake will come near enough to bite him on the portion of his body closest to it, his left wrist, and he'll die for real. As Costigan persuades Murken to go to sleep, he turns out the light in the room. Murken screams. Turning the light back on, Costigan discovers that Murken is dead. There is no sign of injury. Murken's right hand is clenched around his left wrist.

COMMENT
Another first-person narrator named Costigan, this time in a weak story that replicates "The Dream Snake" in its premise of a man whose dream of death from a snake comes true. Howard attempts to provide a psychological basis for Murken's death when the adventurer says that his "dark subconscious mind... will work out the terrible drama as it would have worked out in reality" had he not been rescued. But the nightmarish intensity of the other story is missing, in part because the visible threat

of the cobra is less compelling than that of the unseen and almost hallucinatory menace of the constrictor in "The Dream Snake." This was another tale left unpublished when Howard died, and it might have worked better, revised, as an adventure of his roving troubleshooter El Borak. Fans are gratified to see even these minor works preserved in book form, but they should not be a beginner's first introduction to Howard.

Available in *Pictures in the Fire*

Black Country
First published in *Weirdbook* No. 6, 1973

MAIN CHARACTERS

- Unnamed narrator
- Garo
- Goslanghai
- U'Guno
- Bugbo
- Geshla
- Hausa soldiers

THE PLOT

Upriver of the narrator's African trading post, two chiefs, U'Guno and Bugbo, go to war against each other at the instigation of the rival fetish-men Garo and Goslanghai. Bugbo is victorious after a murderous attack on the enemy village. Fleeing death at the hands of Bugbo's warriors, U'Guno's wizard Garo arrives at the trading post with a mysterious bundle wrapped in monkey skin. He says that U'Guno initially was spared at the insistence of the scheming Goslanghai, who wanted the enemy chief kept alive to counter Bugbo's power. And then Goslanghai went into the jungle "to make magic to see what should be done with U'Gano." There, the witch-doctor was killed and decapitated by an unknown assailant. Unrestrained, Bugbo's bloodthirsty Amazonian wife Geshla then killed U'Gano.

The narrator gives Garo shelter under guard by the post's Hausa soldiers. It transpires that Garo was Goslanghai's murderer, and the dead shaman's severed head was the bundle he carried. Alerted to noises from the room in which Garo is locked, the narrator finds Garo dead from a torn-out throat. His rival's severed head lies beside the corpse, its teeth and lips bloody.

COMMENT

"Black Country" starts with a passage reminiscent of Howard's comments about the west coast of Africa in the letter to Lovecraft noted above. "In that abhorrent land of swamps, black river, nauseous diseases, and mysterious tribes, the Caucasian brain disintegrates swiftly, and men fall prey to strange broodings." This is not the Africa of reality but a fevered Africa out of Howard's dark imagination.

As happened so often with Howard's minor tales (see almost any of the ones surveyed in this guide with 1960s and 1970s publication dates), the main situations in the foreground of the plot are less interesting than the backstories summarized in a few paragraphs. Notably, it's unfortunate that Howard didn't do more with Geshla and her Amazons, whose "tiger-ish ferocity and quickness of thought and action" surpass the abilities of their male counterparts. With more leisure and a surer market, Howard might have been inspired to write a longer and more complicated story, matching Geshla against a swashbuckler like Solomon Kane or El Borak.

Still, if the reader doesn't expect to plunge into a minutely researched, realistic account of tribal life in the French colonies of equatorial West Africa prior to World War II, "Black Country" delivers a fair share of sensational violence and gory horror.

Available in *Pictures in the Fire*

Serpent Vines

First published in *WT50*, 1973

MAIN CHARACTERS

- Unnamed narrator
- Hansen
- Haldred

THE PLOT

Hansen and Haldred seek rare orchids in the jungles of Indochina. Instead, they find a thicket of "cold and slick and clammy" vines that crush Haldred and drink his blood. Hansen escapes and staggers into the narrator's camp, where he tells his story.

COMMENT

Published by Robert Weinberg in a magazine-format, fiftieth-anniversary tribute to *Weird Tales*, "Serpent Vines" is a negligible story that Howard may have intended as the basic material for a longer work. The story ends inconclusively: "God pity mankind if they [the vampiric vines] burst forth upon the world of men!" Perhaps Howard intended to proceed from there with an expedition to destroy the vines, but lost interest first. The story hasn't been reprinted in any of the mass-market paperback collections of Howard's weird fantasy fiction.

Available in *Pictures in the Fire*

Under the Baobab Tree

First published in *Cross Plains*, Fall 1974

MAIN CHARACTERS

- Nukula
- Kesonga
- N-Sunga
- Villagers

THE PLOT

After four lesser chiefs in Chief N-Sunga's village are killed under a nearby baobab tree, their bodies mangled as though by a leopard, the fetish-man Kesonga asserts that the murderer is a demon who takes human shape by day, returns to his true form at night, and leaves grotesque footprints. Telling the young warrior Nukula that the demon is N-Sunga, he dispatches Nukula to slay the chief.

Later, on the way back from the baobab after N-Sunga fails to appear, Nukula escapes death from a spear thrust at him from the underbrush. He strikes back, expecting to see N-Sunga in the thicket, but instead he discovers that his assailant was the treacherous Kesonga. On the witch-doctor's feet are thorn shoes designed to leave monstrous tracks. It was all a plot by Kesonga to seize power by eliminating N-Sunga.

COMMENT

Another throwaway tale, this time presented as horror-fantasy at the outset but concluding with a logical explanation for four murders seemingly committed by a demon. Like the three stories previously surveyed, it saw publication many years after Howard's death, in a limited-edition journal designed for enthusiasts. Aside from its novelty as a Howard adventure populated by an all-African cast of characters, it is too negligible to demand much attention. Still, at the time it was published, when Conan and King Kull had disappeared from the newsstands, such stories as this were welcomed by Howard's growing coterie of fans.

Available in *Pictures in the Fire*

Notes

- "A Thunder of Trumpets" (*Weird Tales*, September 1938) was a collaboration between Howard and Frank Thurston Torbett, a friend and correspondent with an interest in the occult. Set in India, the tale deals with an ill-fated romance between a visiting American girl and a handsome, mysterious Indian, Hanjit, who turns out to be a "Treader of the Path," an immortal student of mysticism. Knowing the girl's love to be futile, the seemingly youthful Hanjit shows her his real appearances—that of an old, old man. The tale is an entertaining one, displaying the influence of Talbot Mundy. Despite the martial connotations of the title, it actually derives from a line in Jack London's novel *The Star Rover*, quoted as an epigraph to the Howard/Torbett story: "For woman *is* beautiful...to man. She is sweet to his tongue, and fragrance in his nostrils. She is fire in his blood, and a thunder of trumpets." It is available in *Pictures in the Fire*.

Faring Town

From the steaming tropics to...where, exactly? Like the de Montour cycle, Howard's short series of tales about a remote fishing village, Faring Town, comprised only two supernatural tales, although the setting also served as a backdrop for one dark but not fantastical poem. This may be another example of Howard becoming enthusiastic about a concept, pouring his creative energy into a story or two, and then moving on to something else, either because he'd lost interest or because he failed to follow the sale of the first story with a sale of the next.

From internal evidence, it's clear that Faring Town exists on a rugged, wind-blown coast somewhere in the northern hemisphere, in the era of "the great sailing-ships that went out on the white tides to brave the restless grey ocean and make ports in strange lands." Beyond that, a particular location is anyone's guess, although the names of two characters, Kulrek and Canool, have a vaguely Inuit sound.

New England, Newfoundland, or even Britain? Take your pick. Equally obscure is the question of whether the setting is the nineteenth century, the eighteenth century, or...? From a reference in "Sea Curse" to a type of galley "still in use among the heathens of Barbary," it might be surmised that the stories take place in the late 1700s, when the pirates of Barbary were still a formidable sea-going power in the Mediterranean.

In the end, such questions hardly matter. Like the haunted African Slave Coast of "squalling teeming life," Faring Town exists more in the realm of Howard's fertile imagination than on any chart or in any maritime history of the real world.

Both "Sea Curse" and "Out of the Deep" have nameless first-person narrators, apparently different individuals. When the "tousle-haired lad" who relates "Sea Curse" describes himself and his friend Joe as "harum-scarum lads of no wisdom," he seems to indicate that he's of about the age and disposition of Tom Sawyer. The narrator of "Out of the Deep" is an older, stronger, more introspective person who may be in his early twenties.

Sea Curse

First published in *Weird Tales*, May 1928

MAIN CHARACTERS

- Unnamed narrator
- Moll Farrell
- Moll's niece
- John Kulrek
- Lie-lip Canool
- Joe

THE PLOT

The niece of old Moll Farrell is seduced by the shiftless bully John Kulrek, and in shame drowns herself. Moll, reputed to be a witch, places a curse on Kulrek and his crony Lie-lip Canool. The two men, Moll says, will be the death of each other: "You shall bring John Kulrek to the doors of hell and John Kulrek shall bring you to the gallows-tree!" she tells Lie-lip. And although Kulrek will be slain at sea, the ocean will not keep his body. The two good-for-nothings depart the next day on a long voyage, and as time passes, Moll grows frailer: "Her eyes smoldered with a light not sane."

Lie-lip returns several months later, and says that Kulrek jumped ship in Sumatra. "There's blood on your hand, Canool," Moll intones. On a rowboat in a dense fog, the narrator and his friend Joe board a galley that has appeared offshore. The ship is decayed, and skeletons sit at the oars. The narrator sees a corpse with a knife in its back. After he and Joe have leaped off, the ship proceeds on into the bay and disappears with a crash, leaving the dead man—the corpse of John Kulrek. Lie-lip confesses that he killed his friend in a brawl and threw him overboard. "The sea has taken vengeance and given me mine," Moll exults before collapsing.

COMMENT

"Sea Curse" is one of the minor weird fantasy stories that kept Howard's name before the readers of *Weird Tales* as Solomon Kane, Kathulos of Atlantis, and King Kull loomed on the horizon. Of itself, "Sea Curse" hardly stands out from the usual run of stories by the magazine's lower-tier writers. Regardless, it will have some interest for Howard fans because of its unusual setting and strongly if economically drawn characters.

The daunting figure of Moll Farrell commands the reader's attention as one of Howard's favorite prototypes: the worn, elderly, but fiercely willful, maternal woman who seems to be afraid of nothing, like Meve MacDonnal in "The Cairn on the Headland," discussed earlier in this guide. Critics who dismiss Howard's writings as one-note macho wish-fulfillment (usually on the strength of cursory or hearsay knowledge) would do well to make the acquaintance of Moll and her memorable sisters.

Kulrek and his pal Lie-lip are the dark side of Howard's roistering characters like Conan and Sailor Steve Costigan: profane, blustering, officious, drunken, violent, and in Kulrek's case, at least, what we would now call sexual predators. There is a fine insight into human nature when Howard describes the townsfolk's reception of the two: "How the cringers and the idlers, the hangers-on, would swarm about the two desperate heroes, flattering and smirking, guffawing hilariously at each nasty jest. For to the tavern loafers and to some of the weaker among the straightforward villagers, these men with their wild talk and their brutal deeds, their tales of the Seven Seas and the far countries, these men, I say, were valiant knights, nature's noblemen who dared to be men of blood and brawn."

And: "...all feared them, so that when a man was beaten or a woman insulted, the villagers muttered—and did nothing." It isn't difficult to imagine that Howard may have drawn on memories of the hardcases who descended on his home town of Cross Plains in its oil-boom period. "I'll say one thing about an oil boom: it will teach a kid that Life's a pretty rotten thing about as quick as anything I can think of," Howard once remembered.

The hell-sent ship conveying Kulrek's body emerges memorably from the fog into the narrator's sight:

> A great beaked prow loomed above us, a weird, unfamiliar shape against the stars, and as I caught my breath, sheered sharply and swept by us, with a curious swishing I never heard any other craft make. ... For from the sides of the ship stood long oars, bank upon bank which swept her along. Though I had never seen such a craft, I knew her for a galley. But what was she doing upon our coasts? They said, the far-farers, that such ships were still in use among the heathens of Barbary; but it was many a long, heaving mile to Barbary, and even so she did not resemble the ships described by those who had sailed far.

Howard might better have left it at that and stopped short of fully revealing the ship's skeletal crew. The image has something of a cartoonish quality that disrupts the misty, foreboding mood that Howard has created, as he himself might have decided given more time to work on the story. But time was a commodity that he had little of in 1928, as he worked furiously to make a living off his typewriter.

Available in *The Horror Stories of Robert E. Howard*

Out of the Deep

First published in *Magazine of Horror*, November 1967

MAIN CHARACTERS

- Unnamed narrator
- Adam Falcon
- Margaret Deveral
- John Gower
- Tom Leary
- Michael Hansen
- John Harper

THE PLOT

The drowned body of young Adam Falcon is washed up on the beach of Faring Town. Strangely, the corpse is covered with a type of seaweed found only at the bottom of the sea. Even more strangely, Adam's fiancée, Margaret Deveral, swears wildly that the dead man is not Adam. That night, Margaret is killed as she sits by Adam's corpse. The body itself vanishes. John Gower, who had once been Adam's rival for Margaret's affections, asserts that a demon reanimated Adam's corpse, and the monster killed Margaret. But the townsfolk suspect Gower of the murder and put him in the stocks while they mount a search for Adam's missing body.

Others are mysteriously killed, including Gower, and one victim before dying swears that the murderer was the reanimated Adam Falcon. A vague idea, perhaps conveyed telepathically by the sea itself, sends the narrator to the beach at dawn, where he confronts Adam's walking corpse. The narrator has guessed or learned by mystic avenues that the true Adam Falcon lies drowned under the sea, and what stands before him is a creature from the ocean depths who has taken Adam's shape. Man and demon fight, and then, slain by the narrator's knife, the creature resumes its real form as "a slimy and moldering mass of seaweed, from which stared two hideous dead eyes."

COMMENT

Where the events of "Sea Curse" take place over a span of months, those of "Out of the Deep" are compressed into one night and the early dawn of the next day. The events of the previous story are alluded to in a reference to "Hangman's Hill, overlooking the bay, [where] Lie-lip Canool's bleached skeleton glimmered against the stars." Depending how long it took to try and condemn Lie-lip for Kulrek's murder, and the rate of his decomposition in the open air after his hanging, the second story may take place anywhere from four months to more than a year after the first one.

Howard nicely builds a mood of mystery and dread as "through the night, horror stalked through Faring town and hunted the sons of men." A swath of "green slime" and seaweed at one murder scene prepares the reader for the final revelation about Adam's walking corpse.

The climactic scene reflects one of Howard's consistent precepts for facing down a supernatural threat. The sea creature or "merman" has easily cut a swath through Faring Town by posing as a man returned from the dead. The townsfolk are easily cowed and murdered: "For what weapon can slay the dead?" But the narrator tells the monster that he has learned its true nature, and knows it "may be slain by a man who does not fear you." Even so, the narrator confesses that he "was never a brave man." Consequently, his decision to confront the monster carries a greater emotional weight than the usual heroics by Howard's herculean characters.

The merman is nicely realized, a menace that last emerged from the ocean depths "so long ago that all men have forgotten the tales." Able to take human form if "lifted from the ocean by the hands of men," it must return to the deep before sunrise; otherwise, presumably, the sunlight will destroy him. In its watery origin and ability to assume human form, it suggests the kelpie of Scots folklore. Even if "Out of the Deep" failed to see print during the author's lifetime, it's surprising that Howard let slide such an interesting concept without retrieving it for another tale.

Available in *The Horror Stories of Robert E. Howard*

Notes

- Before abandoning Faring Town for good, Howard wrote a poem, "A Legend of Faring Town," in which the villagers suspect a secretive old woman, Meg, of infanticide. Mob law ensues, and the villagers learn the truth only too late in the poignant final stanza of the poem. "A Legend of Faring Town" first appeared in *Verses in Ebony*, a 1975 chapbook. It is available in *The Horror Stories of Robert E. Howard*.

Psychic Investigators

Stories about investigators who delve into the supernatural go back at least as far as J. Sheridan Le Fanu's Martin Hesselius, William Hope Hodgson's Carnacki, and Algernon Blackwood's John Silence, and extend up to more recent figures who all seem to be named "Harry": William Hjortsberg's Harry Angel (*Falling Angel*, 1978), Clive Barker's Harry d'Amour ("The Last Illusion," 1985, and others), and Jim Butcher's Harry Dresden (*Storm Front*, 2000, and others).

Additional practitioners include Sax Rohmer with *Brood of the Witch Queen* (1918) and others; Aleister Crowley with *Moonchild* (1917) and others; Jessie Douglas Kerruish with Luna Bartendale, a rare female psychic investigator for her time, in *The Undying Monster* (1922); Dennis Wheatley with *The Devil Rides Out* (1935) and others; Margery Lawrence's Miles Pennoyer; Joseph Payne Brennan's Lucius Leffing; Brian Lumley's Titus Crow; and C.J. Henderson's Teddy London.

These occult detectives or psychic investigators tend either to be private investigators by trade, scholars in obscure areas of learning, or amateur detectives who become involved with the supernatural by happenstance. In Robert E. Howard's regular venue, *Weird Tales*, notable practitioners included Seabury Quinn's long-running Jules de Grandin series, Manly Wade Wellman's John Thunstone, and Pierre d'Artois, created by Howard's friend E. Hoffman Price.

Some Howard fans count most of his stories in modern settings which feature characters named Conrad, Costigan, Gordon, Kirowan, O'Donnel, and Taverel—in various combinations—as an interconnected series about occult investigators who frequent an apparently exclusive retreat called the Wanderer's Club. One Howard collection, *Beyond the Borders* (Baen Books, 1996), includes seven stories that are suggested to comprise most of the presumed series.

Those stories are "The Voice of El-lil," "Casonetto's Last Song," "The Cobra in the Dream," "Dig Me No Grave," "The Haunter of the Ring," "Dermod's Bane," and "The Children of the Night." Three stories not in the same collection but usually included with the others are "The Dwellers Under the Tomb" and two unfinished works, "The House" and "The Jade God." Some speculate that Howard tried his hand in the genre because he was impressed by the popularity of the Jules de Grandin series.

At a glance, it seems reasonable to propose, as these fans do, that Howard envisioned a "Wanderer's Club" cycle with a continuing cast of characters usually centered around an individual named Kirowan. Howard tended to favor series characters, and one of his favorite writers, Talbot Mundy, employed a similar construct in his "Jimgrim" series. There, the central character, James Grim, commands a mostly constant but occasionally fluctuating set of supporting players in quests to root out mystic threats to world peace in India, the Himalayas, and Central Asia.

However, with closer reading, the evidence for an overarching Kirowan series becomes more problematic. The Kirowan who mourns his sister's death in "Dermod's Bane" is named Michael; the Kirowan who boasts a history in occult studies in "The Haunter of the Ring" is named John. The John Conrad of "The Voice of El-lil," "a keen-eyed young New Englander," hardly resembles the studious Conrad of "The Children of the Night" with his "bizarrely fashioned study" housing the *Necronomicon.* One O'Donnel is named John ("The Children of the Night") and another Michael ("The Haunter of the Ring").

Further, some of the stories are more appropriately placed instead in other, more pertinent categories. "The Children of the Night," for example, better fits the category of Howard's weird fantasy stories about the Little People.

Once those considerations are applied, the list of Howard stories in the Psychic Investigator category narrows significantly to six tales, three of them unfinished, that more closely meet the parameters of the genre. Not all of them feature a character named Kirowan. In these completed stories and fragments, the characters address a series of mysterious events that turn out or may turn out to involve what we now would call paranormal or cryptozoological phenomena. In one story, the sleuths are a Gordon, a Kirowan, and an O'Donnel; another, a Conrad and an O'Donnel; a third, a Costigan and a Gordon; an incomplete fourth, a Conrad and a Kirowan; an unfinished fifth, a Gordon; and a fragmentary sixth, a Kirby and an O'Brien.

Did Howard intend one "Conrad," "Gordon," "Kirowan," or "O'Donnel" to be the same as the other, with any inconsistencies attributable to the speed with which he wrote, allowing little time to go back and iron out discrepancies? Or was it simply another instance, repeated in many examples throughout Howard's body of work, of the author's fondness for a particular name sometimes applied indiscriminately to dramatically different characters? Only Howard could have said for sure.

The Haunter of the Ring

First published in *Weird Tales*, June 1934

MAIN CHARACTERS

- John Kirowan
- Jim Gordon
- Evelyn Gordon
- Michael O'Donnel
- Joseph Roelocke / Yosef Vrolok
- Doctor Donnelly
- Bill Bain

THE PLOT

Jim Gordon tells his friends Kirowan and O'Donnel that his wife Evelyn has tried to kill him three times within the past week. Gordon believes that he and Evelyn are the victims of a family curse from three generations back. He can think of no other reason for his wife's aberration. He says he has no enemies; even Joseph Roelocke, with whom Evelyn broke off to marry Gordon, has been friendly toward the couple. The week before, Roelocke sent Evelyn a ring as a belated wedding present, a copper ring shaped like a serpent. Evelyn claims not to remember the attempts on Jim's life, but she is troubled by nightmares of a "horrible faceless black thing that mows and mumbles and paws over me with apish hands."

When Evelyn comes across a gun, her eyes become "dark wells of emptiness" and she shoots Jim. As she recovers and realizes "with grief and terror" what happened, Kirowan collects O'Donnel and confronts Roelocke in his apartment. As he had suspected, Roelocke is Yosef Vrolok, whom Kirowan knew years before "when we delved in the dark mysteries together in Budapest." When Kirowan elected not to "descend to the foul depths of forbidden occultism and diabolism to which you sank," Vrolok spitefully seduced and degraded the woman whom Kirowan loved. Now Kirowan knows that Vrolok jealously tried to "drive Evelyn Gordon's soul from her body," so that it could be possessed by a demon "from *outside* the human universe."

The means by which the occultist attempted to execute his plan is the serpent ring that he gave to Evelyn, "the ancient and accursed ring of Thoth-amon, handed down by foul cults of sorcerers since the days of forgotten Stygia." Because of Evelyn's innate purity, however, the demon could invade her mind only for brief moments. Now Vrolok owes "the price a man must pay for calling forth the nameless shape that roams the gulfs of Darkness." O'Donnel witnesses a "black anthropomorphic shadow" materialize behind Vrolok as he and Kirowan flee. The next day, the newspaper reports the death of Joseph Roelocke from heart failure in his apartment.

COMMENT

In its story of an evil occultist whose own sorcery is turned against him in an instance of justice served, "The Haunter of the Ring" brings to mind M.R. James' classic 1911 horror story "Casting the Runes." On this structure hangs a familiar motif for Howard. By confronting Vrolok, Kirowan avenges the wrong once done to a young woman even as he protects another innocent from a similar fate. Where Edgar Allan Poe once asserted that "the death of a beautiful woman, is unquestionably the most poetical topic in the world," Howard might have added that it's also a strong linchpin for a satisfying revenge story.

Alert readers of *Weird Tales* would have recognized "the ancient and accursed ring of Thoth-amon" as an allusion to the inaugural Conan adventure "The Phoenix on the Sword," which had appeared in the magazine a year and a half earlier. By 1934, Conan had become a favorite of the *Weird Tales* readership, rivaled only by Seabury Quinn's Jules de Grandin. Perhaps Howard had shrewdly decided that he could better his chances of a sale by associating an occult-mystery plot in the Seabury Quinn style with a reference to his own popular sword-and-sorcery series.

In "The Phoenix on the Sword," the master wizard Thoth-amon uses his serpent ring to summon a demon from "the gulf of the Night" to kill his enemy Ascalante. The creature materializes as a shadow whose "outline was not unlike that of a gigantic baboon, but no such baboon ever walked the earth." Presumably, O'Donnel witnesses the advent of the same monster as a "black anthropomorphic shadow" coalesces behind the doomed Vrolok.

Given the revelation that Kirowan and Vrolok once pursued their occult studies in Hungary, readers may regret that Howard overlooked an opportunity to invoke the mythology from "The Black Stone" as an added ingredient in the backstory. Or might it be that the thought crossed his mind, but was rejected because he didn't want to dilute the more timely Conan connection.

"The Haunter of the Ring" is the only story in which Howard's Wanderer's Club is actually mentioned, "composed of the drift of the world, travelers, eccentrics, and all manner of men whose paths lie outside the beaten tracks of life." When O'Donnel says "I had met [Kirowan] at the Wanderer's Club," the reader infers that the organization has a base or residence in the unnamed city where the events unfold, perhaps a refuge of comfortable chairs, soft lighting, good cigars, and strong whiskey, probably all-male and members-only as such clubs were in those days.

Along with the details of cars, traffic, and high-rise apartment buildings, the reference squarely places the story in a modern urban setting far removed from the gothic English estates and remote Transylvanian villages of earlier weird fantasy works by Howard. In the 1940s, writers such as Robert Bloch, Fritz Leiber, and Manly Wade Wellman more and more would set their stories against the same kind of urban back-drop, writing for Dorothy McIlwraith's *Weird Tales* after the retirement of Farnsworth Wright, and for John W. Campbell's *Unknown* magazine.

In this sophisticated twentieth-century milieu, some of the characters are inclined to find a logical, scientific basis for the curse that hangs over the Gordons. O'Donnel scoffs at Jim's notion that he may be the reincarnation of his great-grand-father, doomed to die at Evelyn's hand in retribution for his ancestor's uxoricide. Evelyn's longtime family physician, Dr. Donnelly, attributes her nightmares about a demon to "feminine hysteria."

Another family friend of mature age, Bill Bain, accuses Jim of resorting to "despicable tactics" in laying the groundwork for a divorce by falsely claiming that Evelyn attacked him. O'Donnel initially wonders whether he actually saw a demon begin to materialize in Roelocke's apartment, or had he been hypnotized?

But Kirowan affirms the supernatural reality of Vrolok's scheme:

> No human hypnotism would strike that black-hearted devil [Vrolok] dead on the floor. No; there are beings outside the ken of common humanity, foul shapes of transcosmic evil. Such a one it was with which Vrolok dealt.

In this Howard foreshadows the modern horror architecture of *Rosemary's Baby*, *The Exorcist*, and cable TV "reality" shows like *Ghost Hunters* and *Ghost Adventures*, where medicine, tech-nology, and science come up short in offering a credible prosaic explanation for supernatural occurrences.

Available in The Horror Stories of Robert E. Howard

The Dwellers Under the Tomb

First published in *Lost Fantasies* #4, 1976

MAIN CHARACTERS

- O'Donnel
- Conrad
- Job Kiles

- Jonas Kiles
- The dwellers under the tomb

THE PLOT

Conrad and his guest O'Donnel are awakened late at night by Job Kiles, a miserly old man who lives nearby. Job is hysterical. He swears that his twin brother, Jonas, who died the week before, came to his house that night and peered in through the window. Fearing that Jonas has returned from the dead as a vampire, Job proposes to go to his tomb to see whether his corpse is still there. Conrad and O'Donnel agree to go along, O'Donnel packing a gun as a precaution.

The trio proceeds to the tomb on the lonely Dagoth Hills. As they approach it, they hear a muffled voice crying out for help, which Job identifies as his twin's. Reaching the mausoleum, they find the door still locked and showing no signs of having been disturbed. Job goes in alone, closing the door partially behind him. Conrad, suddenly realizing that Kiles means to pound a stake into his brother's corpse, prepares to follow the old man. Before he can do so, Job screams, rushes out of the tomb, and falls writhing to the ground. He babbles something about "the thing in the coffin" and dies—apparently of a heart attack brought on by a great shock.

Entering the tomb, Conrad and O'Donnel find Jonas Kiles' coffin empty. There is a faint, repulsive odor. A hidden door in the tomb wall opens onto a tunnel in the hillside. Conrad theorizes that Jonas Kiles is still alive, and that he faked death through a self-induced trance. He believes that Jonas may be hiding in the tunnel. He and O'Donnel lay Job's body in the empty coffin and venture into the opening, eventually finding a small chamber containing a cot, cans of food, and a smashed lantern. A diary in Jonas Kiles' handwriting reveal that, as Conrad surmised, Kiles faked his "death." By appearing at Job's window, he would encourage his brother to come to the tomb to drive a stake through his body. At that time, he would kill Job and proceed to pose as his brother.

But it turns out that the family tomb lies over a network of tunnels excavated by a forgotten race. The remnants of these folk still lurk far below, degenerated into "flaming-eyed dog-headed" monsters. Fleeing an attack, Conrad and O'Donnel find Jonas' mutilated body and escape through a door out into the hills, catching a full glimpse of one of their pursuers before the door closes shut. "God protect the sons of men from the Dwellers—the Dwellers under the tombs!" Conrad prays.

COMMENT

"The Dwellers Under the Tomb" was submitted to *Weird Tales* in 1932, but rejected. This seems to have been one of Farnsworth Wright's apparently capricious decisions, since the tale holds up at least as well as many that *Weird Tales* published. Perhaps Wright judged that readers would find the premise and imagery too similar to those of H.P. Lovecraft's "The Rats in the Walls," published in the March 1924 issue and reprinted in the June 1930 issue; "Pickman's Model," published in the October 1927 issue; and "The Lurking Fear," published in the June 1928 issue.

We may assume that Howard read all three stories. He seems to have been particularly impressed by "The Rats in the Walls," writing to Farnsworth Wright in July 1930 that with "the strange and unthinkable bypath into which [Lovecraft] has wandered in this tale," his colleague had "taken a road never traversed, or even dreamed of, by any writer or thinker." Wright forwarded Howard's praise to Lovecraft, initiating a series of correspondence between the two fantasy writers that continued until Howard's death in 1936.

The New England setting in the coastal "Dagoth Hills" demonstrates Lovecraft's influence, underscored by the clear derivation of "Dagoth" from Lovecraft's "Dagon," the name of one of the Cthulhu Mythos entities. As in "The Rats in the Walls," Job Kiles' estate and its ancestral tomb are constructed over a network of passages where one level leads down to another. In "The Rats in the Walls," the different levels documented the survival of a cannibal cult in England from prehistory through the Roman occupation and beyond.

As in "The Lurking Fear," Howard's protagonists discover that the folk who made the passages have degenerated over time, underground, into "the ultimate horror of retrogression." Each successively lower level in "The Dwellers Under the Tomb" indicates another step backward in de-evolution. Lovecraft's subterranean dwellers are the degraded descendants of a reclusive family who from generation to generation have turned into "dwarfed, deformed hairy devils or apes."

Howard's Dwellers have a canine, not simian, appearance, probably drawn from the imagery of "Pickman's Model." There, Lovecraft imagined creatures with a "vaguely canine cast" of features who lurk underneath Boston. The notion seems to have captured Howard's fancy. Nocturnal creatures with "dog-like jaws" also slink through Conan's world in *The Hour of the Dragon*, while in *Almuric*, Esau Cairn saves his sweetheart Altha from monsters who merge simian and canine attributes; they have bodies like those of "deformed apes" and "doglike" heads.

"Pickman's Model" also served as a template for Robert Bloch's "The Creeper in the Crypt" (*Weird Tales*, July 1937) and Robert Barbour Johnson's "Far Below" (*Weird Tales*, June/July 1939), but Howard was there first.

In "Pickman's Model," Lovecraft's described "ant-like armies of the mephitic monsters squeezing themselves through burrows that honeycombed the ground." This imagery is echoed in Howard's story when his protagonists flee through the "mysterious burrows" under the Dagoth Hills to escape the "demonic hordes" that live there. Although O'Donnel packs a powerful .45 pistol ("[c]an't forget your Texas upbringing, can you?" Conrad observes), he and his companion behave like Lovecraft protagonists as they escape the tunnels with a "sob of relief." Then again, even the mighty Conan was "shaken with nausea" when confronted by similar horrors (there called "ghouls") in *The Hour of the Dragon*.

The subplot about Job's fear that his brother has returned as a vampire is a useful piece of misdirection, allowing Howard to refrain from tipping his hand too soon. As in "The Haunter of the Ring," the reader is as much the sleuth as Conrad and O'Donnel are in putting two and two together as Howard introduces each clue about the true horror under the tomb.

Available in *The Horror Stories of Robert E. Howard*

Casonetto's Last Song

First published in *Etchings and Odysseys* No. 1, 1973

MAIN CHARACTERS

- Stephen Gordon
- Costigan
- Giovanni Casonetto

THE PLOT

Opera star Giovanni Casonetto is convicted and sentenced to death after his gory activities as high priest of a satanic cult are uncovered. As he goes to the hangman, Casonetto swears revenge on Stephen Gordon, who accidentally discovered the singer's secret and who was instrumental in his conviction.

Soon after, Gordon receives a package addressed in the satanist's handwriting. Inside is a recording, and a note—also in Casonetto's script—directing that Gordon listen to the recording alone. Suspecting treachery, Gordon's friend Costigan decides to sit in while the recording is played. On the disc, recorded just before the singer's arrest, is Casonetto singing the invocation from the Black Mass. The music sweeps Gordon along, blotting out everything else in the world. He has the illusion of being bound on a sacrificial altar, a dagger hovering over him. As the Black Mass builds to its climax, Gordon feels his mind beginning to shatter. He tries to shut off the phonograph, but he is held helplessly immobile by the incantation. At last, he breaks the spell by screaming, just as Costigan rushes forward and smashes the record.

COMMENT

"Casonetto's Last Song" reads like a vignette that Howard might have dashed off in a half-hour between more demanding work. There is little suspense despite Howard's "hints and glimpses of inhuman voids and unholy dimensions," and virtually no plot complication. Casonetto's use of then-current recording technology to ensnare Gordon is a clever updating of traditional magic lore involving curses and spells. It reminds us that as one who grew up during a time when conveniences like the automobile and the radio came into everyday use,

Howard seemed more comfortable in the surroundings of modern life than his colleague Lovecraft.

The backstory is interesting in its description of Casonetto's infernal temple with its "horned and winged thing to which the devil worshippers bowed." The concept might have worked better had it been expanded at greater length and the background brought to the fore, as a thriller in which Gordon exposes the diabolical priest. It seems possible that Howard may have begun the story as an attempt to write something along the lines of an occult thriller in the Seaury Quinn vein, with some peripheral influence, perhaps, from Lovecraft's "The Music of Erich Zann" (*Weird Tales*, May 1925; reprinted November 1934), then found the material essentially incompatible with his tastes, and quickly wrapped the whole thing up so as to get on to something more to his liking.

Manly Wade Wellman's stories about another occult detective, John Thunstone, which appeared in *Weird Tales* in the 1940s, suggest the sort of thriller that might have resulted had Howard decided to do something more elaborate with his premise. Yet another Costigan appears, this time as a secondary character, although in this tale "Stephen" is another character's first name, not Costigan's.

Available in The Horror Stories of Robert E. Howard

Notes

- "The Jade God," unfinished, combines two characters named John Conrad and Kirowan with a Deep South setting of the kind that Howard enjoyed using. The opening suggests those of "Dig Me No Grave" and "The Dwellers Under the Tomb." Conrad and Kirowan are awakened by screams from the house of their eccentric neighbor, Dormouth. They find Dormouth horribly gashed and torn. He manages to say "the jade god" before he dies. The murderer has escaped, apparently by leaping from the window to a tree in an unusually, and it seems impossibly, long jump. Dormouth's dying words seem to refer to an idol that he had given to Conrad for safekeeping. The fragment ends before the reader can determine whether

Howard intended it to be a supernatural tale or—as seems more likely—a mystery whose seemingly outré element (the murderer's long leap to the tree) turns out to have a rational explanation. It is available in *Tales of Weird Menace*.

- An untitled, unfinished story begins, "The night was damp, misty..." A young woman abruptly enters the London home of the narrator, Gordon, seeking help. She says she's afraid of a snake, and Gordon hears a "faint, slithery sound" outside the door. A man named Falcon, whom Gordon knows, enters. When Gordon says he thinks the girl is "being victimized by a clever mesmerist," Falcon, with her consent, makes hypnotic passes with a dagger. The weapon leaves a symbol on her breast. Gordon suspects "foul magic and devil worship." The fragment ends there before we learn whether Howard meant the story to be supernatural in theme, or a bizarre mystery with a rational explanation at the end. It's also left unresolved whether Falcon will be the tale's villain or not; either way seems possible. The 1,400-word fragment was first published in *Fantasy Crossroads* No. 7, 1976. It is available in *Tales of Weird Menace*.

- "The Spell of Damballah," unfinished, features the occult scholar Kirby and his friend O'Brien. The developing plot is similar but inferior to that of "The Haunter of the Ring." John Ordley seeks Kirby's advice when his fiancée, Joan Richards, apparently falls under the influence of a man who claims to be Ahmed Bey, a wealthy son of a sheik. John's description of a scar on the man's neck seems to interest Kirby. Kirby reveals to O'Brien that "Ahmed Bey" is actually a mixed-race Haitian named Loup who has put Joan under hypnotic influence and plans to eliminate Ordway through voodoo. Kirby confronts Loup at a party at the Richards' high-society home next to the swamplands. Although the story ends before the plot is completely resolved, it appears to shape up as a non-supernatural thriller. The fragment was first published in *Revelations of Yuggoth* No. 1, 1987. It is available in *Tales of Weird Menace*.

Shudder Stories

It was the indefatigable Glenn Lord, the pioneer of Howard studies, who first pointed out Robert E. Howard's contributions to the school of pulp magazines known as "Shudder Pulps" or "weird mystery" magazines. In his cornerstone 1975 study of the genre, *The Shudder Pulps*, Robert Kenneth Jones defined the Shudder school as "a form of mystery story in which the villain perpetrated seemingly supernatural deviltries, which were logically explained at the end."

Typically, Jones said, the magazines featured lurid covers in which women were "pursued down dark corridors, nailed into coffins, whipped, choked, clubbed by cowled fanatics, hunchbacked cretins, gibbering idiots and gnarled seniles." They were the pulpwood equivalent of Paris' notorious Grand Guignol theater, probably better known among Americans in the 1930s than it's remembered today.

Eventually, in the early 1940s, the genre waned. Too many magazines had entered the field, saturating the market and reducing profits for individual publishers whose companies lived and died by newsstand sales. Public tastes changed. Attacks by politicians and self-styled community watchdogs took their toll. The formula of sadism and sex drew the same wrath from the family-values activists of the time as horror comics would in the 1950s, slasher movies in the 1980s, and violent video games today. However, at the height of its popularity in the mid-1930s, the genre promised a reliable, relatively well-paying market for Robert E. Howard as he attempted to "splash the field" and find new outlets for his fiction.

The results were as mixed as Howard's earlier venture into more traditional pulp mystery, which he had exited after two years. Two of his weird-menace stories sold to *Thrilling Mystery*, one of several pulps marketed by Standard Publications and edited by Leo Margulies. These were "Graveyard Rats" (February 1936) and "Black Wind Blowing" (June 1936), both with Texas settings. Two others, "Moon of Zembabwei" and "Black Hound of Death," were accepted by *Weird Tales* after rejection by the Shudders. Another submission, "The Devils of Dark Lake," was also rejected. It appeared years after Howard's death.

Some readers today may look askance at scenes in these stories in which female characters are stripped nude, threatened with torture, and brutally killed, but it was another instance of Howard trying to write to a formula that other pulp authors had found lucrative. Even so, Howard professed to having a difficult time in writing to spec for the market, and the tension is evident where Howard's usual elements of fast action and regional settings strain against and finally burst the weird-mystery template. In regard to the apparent misogyny of the genre, keep in mind that modern movies, TV series, and TV documentaries about psychotic serial killers and violence against women are equally salacious—just more sleekly packaged.

Moon of Zambebwei

First published in *Weird Tales*, February 1935, as "The Grisly Horror"

MAIN CHARACTERS
- Bristol McGrath
- Constance Brand
- John De Albor
- Richard Ballville
- Ahmed ibn Suleyman
- Ali ibn Suleyman
- A torturer
- Zemba
- Cultists of Zemba

THE PLOT
An enigmatic telegram to adventurer Bristol McGrath from his one-time romantic rival, Richard Ballville, brings McGrath

back home to the piney woods of the American South. The message mentioned the name Constance Brand, Bristol's sweetheart, whom Ballville coveted—but Constance was reported dead three years earlier. Hurrying to Ballville's decaying plantation home, Bristol finds his rival's Arab servant Ahmed ibn Suleyman staked out and mutilated. Ahmed dies after scratching a cryptic warning in the dust. Then, at the mansion, McGrath comes across Ballville himself undergoing torture. McGrath kills the torturer, though Ballville himself is already far gone. Ballville reveals that he kidnapped Constance three years before and had kept her a prisoner in the house. Then came John De Albor, a man from Africa whom Ballville met in Europe. De Albor himself lusted after the girl, and turned the local black countrymen against Ballville. Ballville managed to hide Constance elsewhere and send a telegram to McGrath before getting captured by De Albor.

Ballville tells Bristol that the girl is hidden in Lost Cave, a spot McGrath recalls from his childhood. He also warns that De Albor is a priest in the dark African cult of Zambebwei, which worships the apish god Zemba. Then Ballville dies, and a dark man in Eastern garb appears. He claims to be All ibn Suleyman, the brother of Ballville's murdered servant. Telling McGrath that he wishes to avenge Ahmed's death, he follows as Bristol sets out for Lost Cave. At the cave, McGrath finds Constance, and All ibn Suleyman reveals himself to be, in reality, John De Albor. As McGrath sprawls helplessly, paralyzed by drugged brandy, De Albor prepares to make off with Constance. Before he can do so, his former followers abduct Constance to sacrifice her at the full moon, the Moon of Zambebwei, as the Bride of Zemba in a "depraved and bestial" ceremony. McGrath and De Albor perforce team again to rescue her, and once more De Albor double-crosses him. On his own again, Bristol sees De Albor preparing to offer Constance to the god Zemba, a monstrous ape, as the cultists surround him in the ceremony.

When Bristol shoots and wounds the creature, it kills De Albor and scatters the cultlsts. After absorbing more bullets from his gun, the creature seizes McGrath. The Southerner uses his remaining weapon, a man-killing Khyber knife, but the blade proves unnecessary as the ape-god finally succumbs to its bullet wounds. Bristol and Constance are free to start a new life together.

COMMENT

Howard submitted "Moon to Zambebwei" unsuccessfully to *Terror Tales*, "The Magazine of Eerie Fiction!", one of the pre-eminent Shudder Pulps from Popular Publications. Rejected there, it found a home in *Weird Tales* as "The Grisly Horror." The plot contains a little bit of everything from Howard's stable of favorite ideas, including a setting in the "midnight glades" of the Deep South, a menace out of the "grim, hideous jungle" of equatorial Africa, a nude blonde heroine in peril, and a swashbuckling hero who uses the same armament as Howard's Central Asian adventurers. When Bristol executes the "sliding sidewise lunge that slew in silence, severing the throat to the spinal column...a favorite stroke of the hairy hillmen that haunt the crags overhanging the Khyber Pass," it may as well be Francis X. Gordon or Kirby O'Donnell wielding the steel.

In remoteness and savagery, Bristol's American piney woods parallel the "horror-haunted country" of African Zambebwei, which he remembers from past experience. "The river-haunted pinelands were as abysmal in their way as were the reeking African jungles." The black countryfolk whom De Albor recruits into his cult seem almost instinctively to gravitate to the worship of Zemba. "Certain natural conditions produce certain effects," McGrath muses. When the cultists dance to Zemba, they mimic "naked primitive passions framed in a cynical debauchery of motion."

Such passages are likely to rub modern readers the wrong way as barely disguised racism, and if nothing else, they overlook the fact that, then as now, blacks are as devout a community of church-goers as you can find. But Howard was writing for effect, and his imagery isn't far removed from what the average white American typically saw, heard, or read in the misrepresentation of African and African-American life in the mass-media entertainment of his day.

As if trying to outdo himself in devising a system of African-based occult beliefs even more fantastic than voodoo,

Howard proposes that voodoo is only a weak offshoot of "the black, immemorial colossus that had reared its terrible shape in the older land [of Zambebwei] through uncounted ages." Furthering the fantastic aspects of this concept, De Albor enters the ceremony of Zemba wearing "a circlet of gold that might have been forged in Atlantis." The frightful Zemba himself is less a real simian than a lost species out of African cryptozoology—"a monstrosity, a violation of an accepted law of nature—a carnivorous ape."

After the story was rejected by *Terror Tales*, Howard later said, "It's hard for me to write straight formula stuff and make it convincing." "Moon of Zambebwei" may be appreciated best as a sword-and-sorcery fantasy in modern dress. Had it not sold to *Weird Tales* in its present form, might Howard have retooled it as a Conan story? That path was actually taken, although not by Howard, when Roy Thomas adapted it for the *Conan the Barbarian* comic book in 1973.

Available in *Tales of Weird Menace*

Graveyard Rats

First published in *Thrilling Mystery*, February 1936

MAIN CHARACTERS

- Steve Harrison
- Joel Middleton
- Saul Wilkinson
- John Wilkinson
- Richard Wilkinson
- Peter Wilkinson
- Joash Sullivan
- Jim Allison
- Wolf Hunter
- Marshal McVey

THE PLOT

After John Wilkinson is shot to death by Joel Middleton when an old feud flares in Lost Knob, Texas, John's brothers engage a detective, Steve Harrison, to find and apprehend the gunman. Saul, one of the brothers, goes insane when he finds John's severed head on the mantel of their home after the burial. Peter and Richard Wilkinson believe that Middleton has desecrated the grave. But Joash Sullivan, a friend of Middleton's, says John's head was taken from his grave by the ghost of Wolf Hunter, an Indian who had cursed the family in pioneer days.

Harrison digs up John's grave and finds the dead man's headless corpse inside. Then, after glimpsing the apparent apparition of an Indian in traditional garb, he is knocked unconscious. Awakening in Wilkinson's grave, he fights off a horde of flesh-eating rats, said to be the ghost's demonic familiars. He encounters the fugitive Middleton, who admits that he killed John but denies having violated his grave. Harrison says he suspected all along that someone else had taken the head and put it on the mantel, since the evidence pointed to an inside job.

In an old, rat-infested farmhouse as a violent storm breaks, Harrison confronts the man who actually engineered the theft of the head. Richard Wilkinson committed the grotesque act as part of a scheme to grab family property that he wants to lease for oil drilling. As lightning sets the old house on fire, Richard prepares to kill Harrison, but Middleton appears and riddles Richard with bullets, and in turn is shot fatally. Harrison carries the dead fugitive outside as rats swarm over the screaming Richard just before the burning roof falls in.

COMMENT

Howard's semi-fictional Texas town of Lost Knob, earlier encountered in "Old Garfield's Heart," reappears in "Graveyard Rats." The term "semi-fictional" is used advisedly. The description of the area's post-oak landscape replicates that of Cross Plains, Howard's home town, with documentarian accuracy, even if the events of the story are wildly melodramatic. Perhaps Howard set the tale in a familiar milieu because it made him more comfortable in essaying a mystery-thriller, a genre whose formula he never quite mastered.

The weird elements of a phony ghost and ravenous rats pretty much fit the Shudder formula. But how much of the prose is pure Howard? In the magazine version, a long, lurid passage describes Harrison's ordeal after he's knocked out and dumped in the grave, his arm caught in the coffin lid, as the sharp-toothed rats swarm over him with their "squirming, writhing bodies." But the scene doesn't appear in a surviving, partial draft of the story. For that matter, the rats hardly appear either in the draft, and the prose there is quite different (and closer to the rhythms of Howard's usual writing) from the clipped style of the magazine version.

Did Howard rewrite to spec at some point, or did an editor (or someone at the Otis Adelbert Kline agency, which represented him) do the rewriting for him? It's a mystery that even Steve Harrison might find impossible to solve. Harrison was created for a series that Howard wrote for the traditional pulp-mystery market, and then abandoned when he found the whodunit formula incompatible with his style. "Graveyard Rats," perhaps retrieved for the Shudder market, was only one of four Harrison thrillers that sold during his lifetime.

With its stark setting, gothic elements, carnivorous vermin, and macabre imagery, "Graveyard Rats" is likely to satisfy weird fantasy fans. Whether or not they're pure Howard, the horror scenes are effectively painted:

> The lightning flashed oftener and closer, and a low mutter of thunder began in the west. An occasional gust of wind made the lantern flicker, and as the mound beside the grave grew higher, and the man digging there sank lower and lower in the earth, the rustling in the grass grew louder and the red beads began to glint in the weeds. Harrison heard the eerie gnashings of tiny teeth all about him, and swore at the memory of grisly legends, whispered by the Negroes of his boyhood region about the graveyard rats.

Still, the Shudder readers of the 1930s may have noted a missing element. Today's Howard fans may have the same regret: Where is a lissome, naked ingénue who needs to be rescued by the two-fisted hero?

Available in Steve Harrison's Casebook

Black Wind Blowing

First published in *Thrilling Mystery*, June 1936

MAIN CHARACTERS

- Emmett Glanton
- Joan Zukor
- John Bruckman
- Joshua
- Juan Sanchez
- Lem Richards
- The Black Brothers of Ahriman

THE PLOT

On a night of howling wind, Emmett Glanton, a young Texas rancher, is summoned to the home of old John Bruckman, who holds his mortgage. En route he's stopped by Joshua, the recluse's lumbering and mentally impaired but dangerous handyman, who threatens to kill him over something to do with a woman. Warding off the other's attack, Glanton reaches Bruckman's to find that the old man wants the rancher to marry his niece, Joan, promising to tear up the mortgage if he does, with a payment of a thousand dollars in the bargain. Glanton complies when it's clear that Joan wants to get away from her uncle. Joshua is still lurking around. He peers through the window with hate as the couple take their vows. He lusts after Joan.

    Glanton returns to his ranch with Joan, then leaves her with his old Mexican helper, Sanchez, when Bruckman telephones frantically for help. Surviving an attempt on his life by a bizarre character with a ritualistically black-painted face, Emmett finds Bruckman spiked down on a table. The dying man reveals that he had once joined a diabolical cult "in another land," the Black Brothers of Ahriman. The cultists annually sacrifice a young girl and a male closest to her. They have followed him to America, where Joan is to be the sacrifice. Bruckman tried to escape their vengeance by marrying Joan to Glanton, making him the intended male victim.

    Discovering that the Black Brothers have gone on to his ranch to claim Joan, Emmett follows but finds Sanchez gruesomely dead and the girl gone. When he reaches the place of sacrifice, he sees Joan lying nude on an improvised stone altar. The altar and a circle of stones around the clearing are charged with some mysterious form of electricity. Emmett is frustrated in his attempt to reach her, but Joshua charges in, leaping over the electrical field, and decimates the cultists, dying too when he and one of the Brothers are charred as they fall into the energy grid. Glanton and Joan kiss as day finally breaks.

COMMENT
On the checklist of standard elements from the Shudder Pulps, "Black Wind Blowing" contains four features lacking in "Graveyard Rats," notably a "slender, white," beautiful, and nude young woman in bondage: "Glanton almost screamed aloud at the sight. Joan lay there, stark naked, spread-eagled in the form of St. Andrew's Cross, her wrists and ankles strapped securely."

Another ingredient almost but not quite supplied in "Graveyard Rats" when Saul goes mad after seeing his brother's severed head is front and center here: a grotesque, violent lunatic whose "apish figure cavorted and raved like a witch's familiar summoned up from Hell." Thus, Howard feverishly describes Joshua as the madman prepares to assault Glanton on the dark, windy road to Bruckman's.

Modern readers may be inclined to wince at this description of an intellectually challenged man. The readers of the 1930s weird-mystery pulps were probably not, as a rule, as sensitive to such matters as we are today. At that, most readers, even the most socially conscious, would probably react along the lines of Samuel Johnson's famous quote when faced with a similar situation: "If a madman were to come into this room with a stick in his hand, no doubt we should pity the state of his mind; but our primary consideration would be to take care of ourselves. We should knock him down first, and pity him afterwards." Anyway, it's further flavor for a scene in which Emmett and the reader are already on edge from the "black night, with the wind howling under a black sky, whipping the mesquite."

Howard also comes through with a staple of the Shudder Pulps, technology that borders on science fiction, in a "glow from the slag-heaps of Hell," from "boulders [that] had been made conductors of electricity...[with] a voltage terrific beyond his understanding." The boulders and Joan's altar are wired to an "amazingly small, compact, black case-like thing that stood near the altar." Howard provides no further explanation for this seemingly advanced technology in the hands of savage cultists, nor does he need to for this kind of weird fantasy. Of course, "[s]uch a secret could only be evil."

The fourth element of a sinister cult is supplied by the Black Brothers of Ahriman, perhaps inspired by Sax Rohmer's thriller *Fire-Tongue* (1921) or by an obscure 1903 novel, *Dacobra or the White Priests of Ahriman* (1903) by Harris Burland, which also centers on efforts to save a young woman from being claimed by cultists of Ahriman who possess occult or super-scientific knowledge. There seems to be no record that Howard ever read Burland's novel, but the similarities are striking.

The semi-naked, powerfully muscled Brothers are vividly imagined by Howard in a wonderfully pulpish description of the one who tries to kill Glanton in Bruckman's house:

> He was black, but he was not a Negro. He seemed to be stained with some sort of paint from his shaven crown to his finger-tips. And the fingers of one hand were frightfully armed, with steel hooks that were hollow nearly to the points and slipped over the fingers, curving and razor sharp, making terrible, tiger-like talons.

Steel talons have previously been attributed by Howard to an African leopard cult in "Talons in the Dark," first published as "Black Talons" in *Strange Detective Stories* (December 1933).

Where many Shudder stories took place in urban settings, "Black Wind Blowing" returns to Howard's rural Texas and American Southwest roots. Emmett Glanton's name recalls that of Emmett Dalton, the famous Old West outlaw, and that of John Joel Glanton, an infamous scalphunter on the Mexican border in the 1840s. When Howard says that Emmett lives near the town of Skurlock, he's drawing on the name of Josiah "Doc" Skurlock or Scurlock, one of Billy the Kid's gang in 1880s New Mexico. Again, there's the sense that Howard was trying to accommodate himself to the Shudder formula by planting it in surroundings close to his heart.

Available in Tales of Weird Menace

Black Hound of Death

First published in *Weird Tales*, November 1936

MAIN CHARACTERS

- Kirby Garfield
- Richard Brent
- Gloria Brent
- Adam Grimm
- Tope Braxton
- Ashley
- Jim Tike

THE PLOT

Kirby Garfield ventures by night into the backwoods region of "Egypt" to warn a reclusive newcomer, Richard Brent, that a killer named Tope Braxton has escaped from jail and is hiding out in the swamps and piney woods of the area. As he makes his way through the darkness, Kirby hears a deathly shriek. Then a man comes running out of the night and falls at his feet.

Garfield recognizes the man as Jim Tike, who lives on the fringe of Egypt. Tike has been horribly mangled, as though by a wild animal. Before dying from loss of blood, he says that he was guiding a heavily bandaged man through the piney woods to Brent's cabin. The stranger attacked him on the trail because Tike accidentally glimpsed the face under the bandages. Garfield himself is attacked then, but manages to drive off the assailant with his gun.

Kirby pushes on to Brent's cabin. When he warns that two killers are on the loose, Tope Braxton and someone who "rip[s] his victims like a hound," Brent goes into hysterics. Back down the trail, Kirby encounters Brent's servant, Ashley. With Ashley is Brent's niece, Gloria, who has come to the plney woods in response to a telegram supposedly sent by her uncle.

A garbled voice comes out of the dark, mouthing grisly threats. Kirby and Ashley discharge their guns into the trees, with no effect. Back at the cabin, Brent reveals that he is being stalked by Adam Grimm, who accompanied Brent five years before on an expedition into Mongolia. Attacked by the devil-worshipping monks of Erlik, Brent fled, leaving Grimm behind. "Altered" in some way by the diabolists, Grimm has returned to wreak vengeance. Brent fled to the backwoods to elude Grimm—to no avail. Brent thinks Garfield is a spy for his enemy and drives him away again.

Kirby sees a gas bomb thrown into the cabin, and then he is knocked out from behind and regains consciousness in Tope Braxton's custody. The murderer is in league with Adam Grimm, whom he calls "part hound, or wolf." Kirby engages him hand to hand, breaks his neck, and returns to the cabin. Outside lies Ashley, his threat ripped open, and inside Adam Grimm gloats over Brent and Gloria, both of whom are tied down. Grimm tells Brent that the monks of Erlik "altered" him through primitive plastic surgery and glandular surgery, placed "the brand of the hound" on him, and released him. He pursued Brent to the piney woods, and sent Gloria a forged telegram to lure her there as well. He says he will skin the girl to death before Brent's eyes.

Garfield catches his first glimpse of Grimm's face—the jaws elongated to form the muzzle of a hound or wolf, the teeth the fangs of a beast. He fires from the window, riddling Grimm with bullets, but even mortally wounded, Grimm reaches Brent with inhuman vitality and rips out his throat. His vengeance realized, he dies with "a last peal of ghastly laughter."

COMMENT

Rejected by *Thrilling Mystery*, "Black Hound of Death" appeared in *Weird Tales* after Howard's death. Another improvisation by Howard on the werewolf theme, this one substitutes advanced anatomical science for superstition as the explanation for Grimm's terrible condition:

> Those devils [the monks of Erlik] could conquer the world, if they wanted to. They know things that no modern even dares to guess. They know more about plastic surgery, for instance, than all the scientists of the world put together. They understand glands, as no European or American understands them; they know how to retard or exercise them, so as to produce certain results—God, what results!

In the real world, plastic surgery and glandular therapy are hailed today for the benefits they provide. In the 1930s, when the techniques were in their infancy, they were favorite plot devices in the Shudder Pulps to unsettle the reader. Who doesn't fear the scalpel and the needle?

Exploitative nudity also appears, mild compared with today's XXX-rated fare but steamy for its era, when the Shudder and Spicy pulps risked violating federal and state "obscenity" laws by publishing such material:

> Gloria was spread-eagled on a table, held helpless with cords on her wrists and ankles. She was stark naked, her clothing lying in scattered confusion on the floor as if they had been brutally ripped from her.

Now, the greater outcry might come from feminists who decry fiction depicting violence against women.

Adam Grimm lurks unseen for most of the story, leading to the scene in which we and Kirby see his face for the first time:

> Ears, forehead and eyes were those of an ordinary man; but the nose, mouth and jaws were such as men have not even imagined in nightmares. I find myself unable to find adequate descriptive phrases. They were hideously elongated, like the muzzle of an animal. There was no chin; upper and lower jaws jutted like the jaws of a hound or a wolf, and the teeth, bared by the snarling bestial lips, were gleaming fangs. How those jaws managed to frame human words I cannot guess.

Howard's vivid prose produces the chill that horror fans today experience from CGI and cosmetic effects in the movies.

Again, Howard seems to be trying to get comfortable with the Shudder formula by placing it in a familiar setting (as in "Moon of Zambebwei," the piney-woods thickets of the Deep South) with a black-against-white fight-to-the-death that this time pits Kirby Garfield against the fugitive Tope Braxton, "the worst Negro desperado in that part of the state." Again Howard draws from his kit of favorite names, including "Kirby," "Garfield," and "Braxton" for his Southerners and "Brent" for the sophisticates from big-city New York.

In a surprisingly honest insight into American racial attitudes of Howard's day, Garfield says he "always wondered what would be the outcome of a battle between me and Tope Braxton"—but "[o]ne can hardly go about picking fights with black men." At least in the mainstream, such attitudes in

America would change shortly when the professional title fights between black contender Joe Louis and German heavyweight champion Max Schmeling would be played out on the world stage as a symbolic contest between American democracy and the rising threat of Nazi Germany.

As a dedicated boxing fan, Howard would certainly have followed those matches with keen interest. One wonders how he would have regarded the mass-media hoopla over the contests and mulled their implications for the racial content of his stories.

Ironically, unlike Esau Cairn in *Almuric*, who wins his first fight against a larger, more primitive foe by using fisticuffs, Garfield says that strategically applying pugilism against Braxton "would have helped me no more than it would help a man in the actual grip of a gorilla." Although the simile has unfortunate racial connotations, it conveys that the white character has to meet Tope on his own terms by countering his enemy's "blinding speed, tigerish ferocity and bone-crushing strength" with equivalent brute force.

As L. Sprague de Camp once observed, it isn't necessarily a knock against their race when Howard portrays black characters such as Tope as modern-day barbarians. In any Howard story, an honest, elemental barbarian is worth a city-full of civilized decadents. Kirby's savage performance is foreshadowed earlier in the story when Brent disdainfully calls him and the other white gentry of the swamplands "barbarians." "You can talk of barbarians," Gloria rejoins to her uncle, referring acidly to Brent's desertion of Adam Grimm in Mongolia. As in the Conan stories, civilized values are compared with primitive virtues and found wanting.

As in "Moon of Zambebwei" where the Southern American hero wields a Khyber knife, "Black Hound of Death" glancingly conjures Howard's adventures of El Borak when Richard Brent mentions the devil-worshipping "monks of Erlik who dwell in the forgotten and accursed city of Yahlgan." Sinister monks who worship the devil-god Erlik also figure in the Francis X. Gordon, El Borak, story "The Daughter of Erlik Khan," although there their city is called Yolgan.

The monks whom El Borak encounters exhibit no sadistic surgical practices, but they are bad news nonetheless: "Their religion was not a depraved Buddhism. It was unadulterated devil worship." When Richard Brent says that the monks who captured Grimm were "fanatical devil-worshippers," it's clear that they are one and the same as those in the other story, despite the two different ways in which the city is spelled. Howard uses the shared background appropriately for the two stories, giving it a grisly borderline science-fictional twist for one tale aimed at the Shudder Pulps, but eschewing those trimmings for the other one that he hoped to sell to a straight adventure magazine. One wishes that in a perfect world, he could have found a market for a crossover tale featuring both Kirby Garfield and Francis X. Gordon, teaming to fight the globe-spanning scourge of Erlik.

Available in *Tales of Weird Menace*

The Devils of Dark Lake

First published in *WT 50*, 1973

MAIN CHARACTERS

- Steve Gorman
- Rackston Bane
- Joan Grissom
- Dick Grissom
- Celia La Tour
- Bartholomew La Tour
- Esau
- Strozza
- Jeg Buckle
- Bane's servants
- Jack Richards
- Harriet Wilkins

THE PLOT

Steve Gorman receives a frantic phone call from his friend Joan Grissom, who lives with her husband, Dick, also a friend of Steve's, in a cottage near Gorman's home on the shore of

Dark Lake. Driving over to the Grissom cottage, Steve finds the place in shambles and the brutally murdered bodies of another couple, Jack Richards and Harriet Wilkins, lying nearby. Joan is gone. Gorman rushes to Dick Grissom's fishing shack. There, in a strange automobile, he comes upon Joan tied and gagged. The girl reveals that she and Dick are in danger from wealthy Rackston Bane, one of her former suitors. Before Steve can free Joan, he is attacked by Strozza, the Grissoms' former chauffeur and now one of Bane's men, and by a monstrous man ape who knocks him out. The creature, named Esau by Bane, is a specimen from a lost atavistic race in Mongolia.

Steve regains consciousness to find a poisonous spider crouching on his chest. He is saved by Bartholomew La Tour and his sister Celia, two strangers from Haiti. They reveal that Bane has taken the Grissoms to his cabin on Cannibal Island, on the swampy southern portion of Dark Lake. There, he plans to torture them both to death in revenge for his rejection by Joan. The La Tours, a voodoo priest and priestess, offer their help to Gorman. They intend to kill Bane, who betrayed them to a rival voodoo man in Haiti and caused them to flee for their lives.

The three oddly matched allies canoe to Cannibal Island, so named because it was once the refuge of a man-eating killer, Jeg Buckle, now presumed dead and gone. Bartholomew sets out alone to assess the way ahead. A short time later, the canoe floats back down the stream, carrying his severed head.

Celia and Gorman separate to approach Bane's refuge by two different routes. Steve is attacked by the cannibal Jeg Buckle, Bartholomew's murderer, who still lurks on the island. When they fight in the water, alligators seize Buckle, and Steve escapes to rejoin Celia. At Bane's cabin, they find Dick Grissom being scourged by a Chinese torturer. Bane, dressed in a mandarin's robe, forces Joan to watch the grisly scene. Steve prepares to crash in, but before he can do so, Esau appears and again overcomes Gorman. Locked in a hut with a savage dog, Steve kills the canine and outside, encounters another of Bane's servants, whom he fells and whose weapon, an axe, he seizes. Through a window in the cabin, he sees Dick suspended over a serpent pit and Joan about to be subjected to an agonizing death as a hungry rat is placed on her chest, under a heated metal bowl. Celia La Tour is crucified against a wall, but released when Bane stabs her, fatally it seems.

Gorman crashes in and overcomes Esau and the Chinese torturer with his axe. When he throws his weapon at Bane but misses, the madman prepares to shoot him. But Celia, with a dying effort, trips Bane into the serpent pit. There he is bitten to death. Steve frees his friends and sprawls in exhaustion as dawn breaks.

COMMENT

Rejected by the Shudder market, "The Devils of Dark Lake" failed to see print during Howard's lifetime. Like several other tales surveyed in this guide, it finally found a home in a semi-professional publication in the early 1970s, as Howard's popularity began to resurge. It appeared in Robert Weinberg's *Weird Tales* memorial volume, *WT 50*.

Again we see Howard apply the required details of the Shudder Pulps—torture, whipping, snakes, rats, spiders, alligators, rabid dogs, gory means of death, a cultured but insane villain, misshapen functionaries, cannibals, and almost fetishistic female nudity and semi-nudity—to a regional setting. The mixed-race, light-complexioned Celia La Tour is introduced in a state of semi-undress, "in a single garment, low-necked and sleeveless, which did not come to her knees." At the end, the pale-complexioned Joan Grissom is "stretched, stark naked, on a sort of altar."

Bane is served not only by the "shaggy horror" Esau, a Neanderthal from a lost tribe of "monster-men" in Mongolia, but also by "a giant Chinaman" and "a stunted, frizzy-headed black man whose tribal scars indicated that he was a cannibal from the Congo." Howard may have thought that as long as he already had one cannibal in the story with Jeg Buckle, he might as well have two.

The violence is graphic even by the extreme standards of some Howard stories, such as "Xuthal of the Dusk" in which the carnage from one of Conan's sword fights is detailed "with butcher-shop thoroughness," as Fritz Leiber remarked long ago. One of Esau's victims is impaled on a fence picket "whose splintered, blood-drenched tip stood up between her breasts."

Another's head "had been twisted about on its broken neck so that the face looked up between the shoulders." Jeg Buckle had used his remote hut as a "smoke-house wherein he had hanged the severed limbs of the wretches he had murdered and dismembered."

These graphic details are explicit at a level beyond the usual fictional mayhem of Howard's day, at least in mainstream publications. Then, laws set a low bar for judging books, magazines, and movies as salacious and therefore subject to confiscation and often legal action by federal, state, and local regulators. Even when "The Devils of Dark Lake" was finally published forty years later, as films like *The Exorcist* and *The Texas Chainsaw Massacre* were beginning to challenge the limits of censorship already tested by the low-budget cinematic gore-fests of H.G. Lewis a few years earlier, the violence might have been found transgressive by some community standards.

It's as if Howard had determined to give the Shudder Pulp editors what they wanted in sex and sadism (or at least what he thought they wanted) and then some. It may be that the length of the story, not its contents, became the sticking point for the editors of the 1930s. The plot tends to ramble as Steve is overcome by Esau not once but twice, and the addition of the cannibal Jeg Buckle adds an arguably extraneous subplot. Howard devotees are happy when the author delivers two fights where one would normally do, but in the 1930s, he was another workaday pulp writer trying to score with markets (like the Shudders) that often had already developed their favored stables of steady contributors who could write faithfully to formula.

The story seems not to have been submitted to *Weird Tales* as a fallback market. Had it been, its length and extreme violence may have worked against it there, too. Ironically, it was one of the more satisfying of Howard's previously unpublished, non-series stories to emerge in the early 1970s because it was longer and more substantial than the slighter tales that were published around the same time, like "The Horror in the Night" and "Under the Baobab Tree."

Available in Tales of Weird Menace

Note on Current Sources

The following publications are the most recent in which the stories surveyed in this guide are available in pure-text form as Howard wrote them—or, in the absence of surviving manuscripts, as they were originally published. The discussion of each story notes in which specific collection the story can be found:

- *Adventures in Science Fantasy* (REH Foundation Press, 2012)
- *Bran Mak Morn: The Last King* (Ballantine Books/Del Rey, 2005)
- *The Horror Stories of Robert E. Howard* (Ballantine Books/Del Rey, 2008)
- *Pictures in the Fire* (REH Foundation Press, 2018)
- *Sentiment: An Olio of Rarer Works* (REH Foundation Press, 2009)
- *Steve Harrison's Casebook* (REH Foundation Press, 2010)
- *Tales of Weird Menace* (REH Foundation Press, 2010)
- *Western Tales* (REH Foundation Press, 2013)

For those interested in tracking down other appearances, the invaluable web site "Howard Works" exhaustively lists every magazine, journal, softcover, and hardcover publication of every Robert E. Howard story. It is an indispensable resource for Howard fans, whether newcomers or veteran enthusiasts.

About the Author

Fred Blosser is a long-time historian of Robert E. Howard. His articles, critiques, and observations about Howard and his work appeared in the Marvel Comics magazines *The Savage Sword of Conan*, *The Conan Saga*, and *Kull and the Barbarians*, as well as in the semi-professional journals *The Howard Collector*, *The Howard Review*, *The Dark Man*, and *Cross Plains*. He has also appeared in *Cinema Retro*, *Amra*, *Crypt of Cthulhu*, *The Dark Side*, *Savage Tales*, *Mystery Scene*, and *The Armchair Detective*.

Blosser is the author of the "Informal Guide to Robert E. Howard" series of scholarly works, which currently include this volume and its three predecessors, *Western Weirdness and Voodoo Vengeance*, *Ar-I-Ech and the Spell of Cthulhu*, and *Silken Swords*, as well as *Savage Scrolls: Volume One*, all from Pulp Hero Press.

www.ingramcontent.com/pod-product-compliance
Lightning Source LLC
Chambersburg PA
CBHW052041090426
42739CB00010B/1997